To my brother Eric,
my first partner in Normandy Landings strategy games.

BENOÎT RONDEAU

Airborne Operations for the Normandy Landings

Editions OUEST-FRANCE

PROLOGUE

"Hold until relieved"

00:16, June 6th 1944 Horsa glider number 91, decorated with chalk, flown by Jim Wallwork, had just finished its mad career into the barbed wire protecting the German defences of the Bénouville bridge, which spanned the Orne Canal. The landing was exceptionally accurate: Wallwork arrived at the objective. Nine minutes earlier, the six Horsas of

Major John Howard commanded the airborne troops who seized Benouville bridge.

Operation Deadstick - the *Coup de Main Party* - were released from the cables of their towing aircraft. One hundred and eighty élite troops, overloaded with arms and equipment, were on board.

They were commanded by Major Howard, a talented officer who was entrusted with one of the most perilous, the most essential and the most famous of the D-Day missions. Its target was the capture of two bridges which the 6th British Airborne imperatively needed to secure before the coastal landing began. The Bénouville bascule bridge, codenamed *Euston I* for *Operation Overlord* - the invasion and the liberation of Europe - would go down in history as *Pegasus Bridge*, referring to Pegasus, the winged horse of Greek mythology and the emblem of the British airborne forces. On the Orne, the

The bridge has gone down in history under the name of 'Pegasus Bridge'. This panel is the original, which was located at the entrance to the bridge in 1944.
Coll. Tanguy Le Sant

A perfect landing! An ingenious system allowed the rear of the Horsa to be separated from the rest of the fuselage, allowing vehicles or artillery to be unloaded. NARA

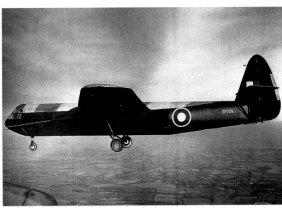

With its silent approach carrying twenty-eight soldiers, the Horsa glider was ideal for carrying out a _coup de main_. Royal Air Force

second bridge which Howard had to seize, codenamed _Euston II_, was not far away from the first.

The gliders slipped silently through the Normandy night, gracefully turning to their new heading. The pilots, who had repeatedly practised the manoeuvres, were busy with their flight plans: quickly checking their watches, compasses and wind speed. But, soon, like silver ribbons in the dark of night, the two waterways came into the view of the pilots and co-pilots. On board, the men, who had fallen silent after singing a few songs, were now preparing for imminent impact: their landing would be rough. The descent was rapid, so they yelled loudly to avoid the possibility of deafness caused by the abrupt change in pressure. There was no longer time to turn back: this time, it was the real thing. The invasion, for which these men had meticulously prepared themselves for so long: at last.

The landing of a troop-carrying combat glider was no easy matter, especially when the operation took place in enemy

territory. Sitting up front in their wooden cockpits, the pilots risked their lives, just hoping for nothing worse than a few broken limbs. However, the speed of Howard's glider, No. 1 - which soldier Wally Parr had christened _Lady Irene_, after his wife - was excessive. Wallwork came in very fast, landing on the soil of Normandy at 150 km an hour. The glider burst through the first barbed wire defences. "Stream!" he ordered Ainsworth, who activated the parachute brake. The tail tilted up abruptly: their speed fell to less than 100 km an hour, but all the wheels were broken and the wooden skids placed under the fuselage sent up sparks. Relieved of its parachute, the glider finally came to rest. Howard lost consciousness for a few seconds. Coming to, he could not distinguish anything: had he gone blind? No; it was simply that his helmet had slid down over his eyes ... But already the second glider, No. 93 was coming in. Fearing to crash into the first glider, the pilot, Boland, manoeuvred to avoid it, resulting in its fuselage breaking in half. The third glider,

Duly trained, the airborne troops were formidable fighters. It only took them a few minutes to seize the Bénouville and Ranville bridges. IWM

A landing zone was laid out near Ranville during the night of June 5-6. Howard's men had to be reinforced as quickly as possible. IWM

No. 92, landed in its turn, near a pond, the existence of which had not been suspected, two minutes after Major Howard: it was then 0:18 am. How was the landing beside the Orne? Glider No. 95 came in far too quickly. The opening of the rear doors, the parachute brake: nothing worked. It could not land right beside the bridge and slid noisily along the ground, a few metres from the objective: Lieutenant Sweeney hitting the cockpit heavily in the process. The sixth glider in the *Coup de Main Party*, No. 98, on the other hand, made an outstanding, exemplary landing. The pilot, Roy Howard, had only to turn and announce to Lieutenant Fox that they had arrived. As for the last glider, Captain Priday's, it ended up more than 13 kilometres to the east ...

The fighting had already begun. Incredibly, all the commotion made by the gliders' landing did not alert the Germans. In any event, the airborne troops were both quick and lively. Lieutenant Brotheridge ordered the Bren gunner to

get out quickly. They charged flat out, taking the enemy by surprise. The most important thing was to silence the bunker to the north-east of the bridge. Its fate was settled in a matter of minutes. While the men worked to clear the trenches on the right bank, near the landing site, a few soldiers led by Brotheridge, who had just shot a German, were crossing the bridge. Almost across, the Lieutenant was fatally wounded in the neck and collapsed. His men silenced the enemy positions.

Lieutenant Wood's men from glider No. 93 and Lieutenant Smith's group from glider No. 92 came running to join the action. The firing continued: shouts and screams mingled with the sounds of gunshots and explosions. In the confusion, two French civilians, Auguste Delaunay and Alexandre Sohier, were killed by mistake. A tragic fate which might well have happened to Georges Gondrée, who rashly went to his window, only to receive a burst of machine gun fire from the Sten of Lieutenant Smith, who was a little too fast on the trigger. Louis Picot who, like Georges Gondrée, ran a café, was less fortunate than his compatriot: he was unable to stop himself cheering the liberators with a resounding "Vive les Anglais!". He was killed outright by a burst fired by a German, posted under his terrace. As for the charges believed to be placed under the bridge, Captain Neilson's sappers, of 249 Field Company Royal Engineers, found no trace of them: although the wires had been put in place by the Germans, the demolition charges were discovered later in a nearby hut.

At 0:21 am, five minutes after the first landing, the crews of Howard's three gliders had fulfilled their mission: *Euston I* was under their control; the defences were eliminated. The losses were minimal. Among the dead, David Wood, who had been trapped in the wreckage of the second glider in the pond, had drowned. What had happened beside the Orne bridge? No sooner had they arrived, than Fox and his men leapt out of the glider and without a fight had taken the lightly defended bridge; the ineffectual firing from a German machine-gun was quickly neutralised by Sergeant Thornton's precision mortar fire. Shortly afterwards, they were joined by Lieutenant Sweeney's group. When the latter asked about the situation, Fox replied with a very British sense of humour: "The exercise went very well, but I can't find a blasted referee to decide who is dead and who is alive!" Fox then sent two dispatch riders to Major Howard to report the success of the mission. The latter was greatly relieved. He immediately ordered Corporal Tappenden, his radio operator, to

The gliders also allowed heavy equipment to be conveyed, which would have been needed in case of Panzer counter-attack. IWM

send the message informing his superiors that everything was going according to plan. This message was contained in the codewords: 'Ham' and 'Jam', signifying the capture intact of the Bénouville and Ranville bridges respectively. To let his whole team know of the success of *Coup de Main*, Howard whistled a 'V for Victory' in Morse, which was very reassuring for the group. Howard and his handful of combatants had only just begun their day. Heavy fighting lay ahead, in perhaps the hardest phase of their mission. "You will hold until relieved", were Howard's orders.

The airborne operations of the Landings began with this spectacular raid, which represented only one aspect of a particularly complex operation, carefully planned and carried out with massive resources.

PREPARATIONS FOR THE D-DAY AIRBORNE OPERATIONS

AIRBORNE OPERATIONS IN OPERATION OVERLORD

Planning an airborne operation is complex: landing zones had to be established for the gliders. IWM

Preparations for an airborne operation are particularly complex. A large number of factors and constraints have to be taken into consideration. In addition to the training of troops involved, and the close coordination required between the different units, it has to provide answers to a multitude of questions: what are the objectives? What will be the aircraft's flight plan? Which dropping zones (*DZ*) will be used for airdrops? Which landing zones (*LZ*) will the gliders use? How should the take-off timetables be organised? How should the

The C-47, gone down in history as the Dakota in its civilian version, was the airborne allies' war horse. Coll. Tanguy Le Sant

THE PARAS' AIRCRAFT ON D-DAY

Better known as the Dakota or DC-3 in its civilian version, the C-47 Skytrain could carry twenty-eight paratroops. For jumping, a hatch had been fitted in the fuselage of an Albemarle, originally designed as a bomber, not for dropping paratroops. On board this aircraft, space was limited; only ten paras could be carried lying down, as it was impossible to stand up. Each time that the dorsal turret gunner moved position, the men had to move. Faced with the need to carry large and varied loads of equipment, to compensate for the lack of space in the aircraft, they attached canvas bags (*Parapacks*) under the wings. Albemarles, Stirlings (of which the Mark V could carry forty paras) and Halifaxes were assigned to towing gliders.

supplies be organised? What are the ways to mislead the enemy? The maximum possible information must be gathered on the objectives and the enemy's dispositions; tactical plans must be produced and revised in the light of new information. Certain limits are imposed on the planners: the number of aircraft, the number of men, the space available in the gliders, the date chosen for the operation ...

Dispersal was one of the main hazards of airdrops. Should they, therefore, have used more gliders? IWM

The unknown quantities

The choice of timing for the airdrops was crucial. The D-Day airdrops were the first to be carried out at night as part of a major operation: the airborne troops had to reach their objectives before dawn, the time set for the start of the amphibious assault. Although aircraft and paratroops made less visible targets at night, finding the *DZ*s and *LZ*s was much more difficult. The choice of these zones was one of the critical decisions. It had to take into account the proximity of the objectives; the presence or otherwise of enemy forces; the suitability of the terrain for landing gliders or paratroops; the ease of organising assembly points on those zones; as well as the availability of communicating routes for moving around. The advantage of a Drop Zone at a distance from the objective was in avoiding possibly disastrous enemy fire when dropping directly over the target. However, the speed of the action could take precedence. In this case, the silent glider represented the ideal solution. In addition, it had the great advantage of allowing the troops to go directly into action and preventing the dispersal inherent in a parachute drop. On the other hand, the Allies would need a moderate wind speed for the airborne operation and low cloud cover.

Soldiers carried by 82nd Airborne US gliders cross the aerodrome tarmac, heading for their gliders.
They all wear Mae West lifejackets, like the cabin crew.

Ike and Monty broaden the airborne operation

In the first plan, drawn up by COS-SAC (Chief of Staff to the Supreme Allied Commander, headed by Lieutenant-General Morgan) in August 1943, dropping two- thirds of an airborne division over Caen was envisaged, directly opposite the beaches where three divisions were to land, between Grandcamp and the mouth of the Orne. It was agreed that the optimal use of lightly armed airborne forces was to be deployed on the flanks of the invasion, so as to secure the most exposed parts of the amphibious assault zone. The revision of the plan by the general staff of SHAEF (Supreme Headquarters Allied Expeditionary Forces), which had absorbed COSSAC and which was headed by General Eisenhower, completely changed the planned deployment of the paratroops. While General Marshall pressed Eisenhower to use the airborne division boldly, by dropping them between Dreux and Évreux to delay the arrival of the German army reserves, the SHAEF commander pointed out that this would be a suicidal mission (the airborne troops, deprived of support other than by air, would be swept away by the Panzers) and the priority was to secure the immediate rear and flanks of the landing zone. Three airborne divisions of the 1st British Airborne Corps and the US Army were by now involved in *Operation Overlord*, which was extended to the Cotentin. It was understood that they would be reinforced as soon as possible by units, specially assigned to this task, landing by sea.

The paras would need the immediate support of reinforcements landing on the beaches: elements of the 4th US ID (notably Task Force Raff, essentially made up of elements of the 82nd US Airborne) for the Americans and, for the British, commandos from the 1st Special Service Brigade under Lieutenant-Colonel Lord Lovat.

Last minute changes

The available aircraft did not have the capacity to transport the entire three airborne divisions in a single trip, so the paratroop drop and the arrival of the gliders occurred in several phases. Some units were even taken by sea. The plans were subjected to several revisions: in the British sector, it was originally planned to entrust the nocturnal missions to one parachute brigade and have a second brigade land from gliders. But the discovery of fields covered with wooden stakes ('Rommel's asparagus') forced the planners to renounce the use of gliders in a massed night landing: instead, they would first drop two airborne brigades. For a time, the Americans also considered using massed gliders for the first wave: Lieutenant General Bradley,

commander of the 1st US Army, wanted 75% of his force to be landed from gliders, so that he could concentrate his forces more easily. Major-General Ridgway, who commanded the 82nd US Airborne, also wanted to use gliders to deploy their artillery pieces quickly. However, the mass deployment of gliders was called into question during the second half of April, after many accidents occurred during exercises. On April 28, it was finally decided that the initial assault would be entrusted to the paras.

A significant change to the plan was made on May 26, after the Resistance reported an increase in the number of German units stationed in the Cotentin. The 82nd US Airborne, which originally was to be parachuted into the Saint-Sauveur-le-Vicomte area, risked being isolated and annihilated. Consequently, Bradley decided that it would go into action more to the east, from the other side of the Merderet to Sainte-Mère-Église (until then the objective of the 101st). Ridgway and his counterpart in the 101st, Taylor, accepted this change: the strengthening of the German defence forces did not in any way mean that their divisions would not be capable of successfully carrying out their missions. Although the changes affecting the 101st were minor, the plan involving Ridgway and his 82nd was profoundly affected. The divisional officers were appalled at this last-minute change: for months they had been studying in

Choosing to carry out airdrops by night meant that the moon had to be favourable. To coordinate properly with the amphibious landings, the tide also had to be taken into account. IWM

The Waco, known as the CG-4A, was an American glider. It could carry fifteen airborne troops, a jeep or a piece of artillery.
US Air Force

THE D-DAY GLIDERS

Three types of gliders were deployed in Normandy: the Airspeed Horsa, the Waco CG-4 and the General Aircraft 49 Hamilcar. The Horsa, designed by Hessell Tiltman and built entirely from wood, was given the revealing sobriquet 'Flying Coffin'. It was also called the 'Flying Matchbox'. Weighing nearly 7 tons fully loaded, it could accommodate twenty-eight soldiers, or a lightweight vehicle and artillery. The Waco had canvas-covered wood and metal frames. Used only by the Americans, it carried only fifteen men, a light vehicle or artillery. The Hamilcar was the largest glider used by the Allies (only by the British). Its carrying capacity allowed it to transport a seventeen pounder anti-tank gun or a Tetrarch light tank.

detail the photographs and maps of their assigned objectives and, suddenly, they learned that all their planning and training had gone by the board.

It was also at the end of May that another change was made which would affect the 82nd and 101st US Airborne. The first two American glider transport

GIs of the 82nd US Airborne getting ready to board their gliders: they risked crash-landing, without the incentive of the $50 paid to paratroopers for each combat jump carried out! NARA

missions, *Operations Detroit* and *Chicago* were brought forward from first light to about 04:00, just before dawn, to give greater protection against anti-aircraft fire. The officers of the C-47 squadrons and glider units involved in these operations protested against the idea of changing to night landings. The only concession given to them was to use American Waco gliders, judged more manoeuvrable than the British models. This, however, required a rapid revision of the plans and a substantial reduction of the material transported; and all this just a few days before D-Day.

Leigh-Mallory wanted to cancel the operation

Sir Trafford Leigh-Mallory predicted heavy losses within the airborne divisions.

Other difficulties arose. Air Marshal Leigh-Mallory, commander-in-chief of the air forces and therefore responsible for airborne operations, ended up opposing the plan which had been accepted by a unanimous consensus. A real Cassandra, he predicted losses which could have risen to 70% of the American airborne forces to be dropped on the Cotentin Peninsula. The losses would be too high for the results achieved. Eisenhower could not endorse Leigh-Mallory's recommendations: the airborne phase of the *Neptune* plan simply had to succeed. In his eyes, as well as those of its planners, it was an essential element for the success of the landing on Utah, and thus for the success of the Landings as a whole.

CHOICE OF UNITS

The British committed a division on D-Day the 6th Airborne (here, elements of the 6th Airlanding Brigade). IWM

THE ALLIED AIRBORNE FORCES

The airborne assault would therefore be carried out by the 6th British, 82nd and 101st US Airborne. The Americans of Major-General Williams' IXth US Troop Carrier Command and two groups from the RAF, Nos. 38 and 46, commanded by Air Vice-Marshal Hollinghurst, were assigned to the transport of these airborne forces. Lieutenant-General Boy Browning, who commanded the Allied airborne forces (except the 82nd and 101st US Airborne), had available the following forces: 1st and 6th British Airborne Divisions, Polish Parachute Brigade, two French SAS paratroop battalions, the British SAS brigade and Norwegian, Dutch and Belgian paratroop companies.

The *Red Devils*

On April 23, 1943, the War Office had decided to create the 6th Airborne. The command was entrusted to Major-General Gale, who gave the division its motto 'Go To It!' Fully trained and rigorously selected, the British paratroops - who had adopted the nickname of *Red Devils* given to them by their adversaries during the Tunisia campaign - were conscious that they constituted an elite unit with a strong feeling of camaraderie. This identity was emphasised by the wearing of uniforms specifically for airborne units: the maroon beret, officially recognised on July 29, 1942 (one version of the choice of colour attributes it to Daphne Du Maurier, Browning's wife) and the camouflage battledress, the Denison Smock. Their first exploits, and the reputation gained by the paratroops, contributed to forging their esprit de corps. The unit's emblem was the soon-to-be famous Pegasus. However, like their American counterparts,

Major General Gale, the energetic commander of the 6th Airborne. IWM

British paratroops had a strong tendency to look down on and discredit their comrades of those airborne units transported by gliders. The latter were not volunteers and the paras believed, quite wrongly, that a landing in a glider was free from danger, as compared to an operational jump. In a wry play on words, the paras called them the Chairborne Airborne.

Gale and some of his men of the 5th Parachute Brigade, shortly before boarding for Normandy. The general knew how to prepare them for their missions. IWM

Perseus astride the winged horse Pegasus: the emblem of the British airborne forces, which was chosen by the novelist Daphne du Maurier, wife of General Browning, 'boss' of the British airborne troops.
Coll. Tanguy Le Sant

6TH BRITISH AIRBORNE

With a complement of 12,500 men, this included two Parachute Brigades, Brigadier Hill's 3rd (which relied on Canadian paratroops) and Brigadier Poett's 5th, and Brigadier Kindersley's 6th Airlanding (airborne) Brigade.. The usual support troops completed the organisation of the division, including 100 anti-tank guns, 27 howitzers and an armoured reconnaissance regiment with 11 Tetrach light tanks.

The airborne troops were among the few British soldiers to wear a camouflage uniform (the 'Denison Smoke') as well as a specially adapted helmet, different from the famous tin helmet.
Coll. Tanguy Le Sant

The Screaming Eagles

The 101st US Airborne Division (named the '*Screaming Eagles*' after its divisional insignia) was created on 15 August 1942. The American airborne forces recruiting teams were particularly on the lookout for dependable young men for this highly specialised branch of the army. Stalwart and psychologically suitable men were required to serve within an élite unit. Volunteers, the American paratroops received a premium of $50 for each combat jump. The men transported by gliders did not benefit from this supplementary pay, an injustice which was put right in July 1944. The men of the Glider Regiments were dubbed the 'glider riders' by their parachuting comrades, even though they were much more boisterous. The Americans adopted a practice unique in the armed forces of the belligerent countries: before leaving for Normandy, the GIs subscribed to a $10,000 life assurance policy. The first combat test for the *Screaming Eagles* was none other than *Operation Overlord*, as until then the unit had never been under fire, unlike their comrades of the 82nd US Airborne. In February 1944, very suddenly, its commander, General Bill Lee, the father of the American airborne unit, suffered a heart attack. Against all expectations, it was not his second-in-command, Brigadier-General Don Pratt, who succeeded him but Major-General Taylor.

Major General Maxwell Taylor, commander of the 101st US Airborne. Caen Memorial

Before his departure, Lee organised transfers between officers and non-commissioned officers of the 101st with those of the 6th British Airborne, which was in camp south of the Americans, on Salisbury Plain. The exchange of ideas and techniques proved fruitful. However, a major fight broke out at Devizes, involving five hundred men. It took no less than three sections of MPs to cool the combative ardours of the participants.

The insignia of the 101st US Airborne, which gave its men the nickname of 'The Screaming Eagles'. Coll. Tanguy Le Sant

Beside
A typical D-Day para, complete with his harness, anti-gas armband and first-aid kit. Coll. Tanguy Le Sant

Below
The American paras had a chest parachute, completely useless, as well as, very often, a 'legbag'. Coll. Tanguy Le Sant

101ST US AIRBORNE

For *Overlord,* the division had three paratroop regiments - the 501st (Colonel Johnson), 502nd (Colonel Moseley) and 506th (Colonel Sink) PIRs (Parachute Infantry Regiments) and the 327th Glider Regiment (Colonel Wear) - as well as many support units. Harper's 401st Glider Regiment, initially attached to the 101st, was then divided between the 325th and 327th Glider Regiments (to which it provided a third battalion).
The division had a total strength of 9,000 men, nearly three hundred jeeps, one hundred lorries, about a hundred mortars, thirty-six 75mm howitzers and anti-tank guns. The division was transported by the aircraft of the 435th and 439th Groups.

The All Americans

The first American airborne division trained at Fort Benning was General Ridgway's 82nd US Airborne. The unit saw successive action, in 1942 in North Africa, in 1943 in Sicily and then in Italy, with more or less success. However, this was a highly desirable battle experience for a unit selected to take part in the early phases of *Operation Overlord*. In February 1944, the 505th was based at Camp Quorn, Braunstone Park, near Leicester, a city in which the GIs of the 82nd were involved in a number of fights, sometimes between Americans. Ridgway deplored some racist incidents which could have reflected badly on the men and he made it a point of principle to explain to each of the units that all Americans, including African-Americans, wore the same uniform. Feelings were also running high with the British soldiers. It has to be said that the soldiers from across the Atlantic, particularly those wearing the insignia of the paras, caught the eye of the young English women (at last, girls who speak English, noted the veterans of Africa and Italy, with relief). The 507th and 508th PIR were based near Nottingham. The tents of the 508th (even though each one had a stove and a paved and cemented base) were pitched in Wollaton Park. It was reported that the owner did not take kindly to an American para killing a deer

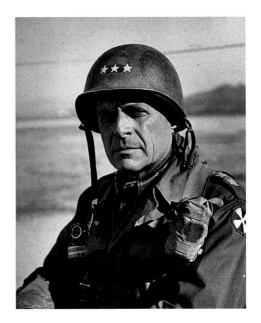

Matthew Ridgway headed the 82nd US Airborne NARA

on his land. Coming back to D-Day, in order to be identified by the French, and to avoid any murderous reaction by the enemy if they thought they were dealing with commandos - who were to be shot, according to Hitler's 1942 order - the US paratroops of the 82nd Airborne wore an American flag on the right sleeve of their uniform. Some authors claim that a few elements of the 101st were similarly equipped, but this seems doubtful.

**The 82nd Airborne, called 'All Americans',
because its members were supposed to come from
all over the United States.** Coll. Tanguy Le Sant

82ND US AIRBORNE

For D-Day, the 9,000 strong unit was divided into three paratroop regiments - the
505th (Colonel Ekman), the 507th (Colonel Millet) and the 508th (Colonel Lindquist) PIR - and a glider regiment, the
325th (Colonel Lewis), not including the
support units. Only the 505th had combat
experience. Colonel Tucker's 504th, the
other PIR attached to the 82nd Airborne,
was still deployed in the Mediterranean.
It did not reach England until May in
1944, too late to take part in D-Day, except for some of its members who joined
the ranks of the Pathfinders (only 28
jumped over Normandy).

**Special helmet, Jump Outfit 42 and national
identification flag: the uniform of an officer
of the 82nd Airborne on June 6, 1944.**
Coll. Tanguy Le Sant

THE PATHFINDERS

Hard men for a perilous mission

The Pathfinders were the guides of the airborne divisions. They were the vanguard of the invasion, whose mission was to prepare for the airdrops by marking the *DZ* and *LZ*. It was decided that there would be sixteen or eighteen men in each team, or stick. It remains a fact that success depended largely on good navigation by the pilot making the drop, which was not always the case. The 82nd and 101st counted three hundred and eighty Pathfinders transported in twenty C-47s, while sixty British Pathfinders, aboard six Albemarles, were involved on D-Day.

Pathfinders of the 6th Airborne set their watches. On the left, Lieutenant de la Tour, killed in Normandy. NARA

Specialised hardware

One clever piece of direction-finding apparatus designed by the British consisted of a Eureka beacon emitting a radio wave to guide a device with a Rebecca receiver (the name was chosen by Browning, in tribute to his wife's most successful novel (Rebecca, by Daphne du Maurier). The Pathfinders also used AN/UPN radar (which weighed almost 60 kilos) which emitted a very high frequency radio signal which could be picked up by aircraft equipped with SCR-717 radar which showed details of the ground surface on a screen. The third way to locate the position of a plane was GEE, a radio triangulation system using three transmitters based in England. The Eureka/Rebecca system, while far from perfect, was the most effective, but it was only used by the leading aircraft, in order to avoid Eureka beacon saturation. To guide the aircraft at night, the pathfinders also had Holophane or Aldis lamps: each regiment was assigned a specific light colour. These lamps, seven in number, were laid out in the form of a 'T'. At the same time, a Morse signal was sent, identifying the *DZ*, so that for *DZ* A the letter 'A' was used. They were placed so as to be seen from the sky while remaining invisible on the ground. Keler lamps were also used, mounted on poles. The Pathfinders also had Very pistols, using different colours to identify the jump zone for aircraft on approach. No radios were provided for direct voice contact between the Pathfinders and the aircraft carrying the paratroopers.

The Eureka beacon: essential equipment for marking the jump zones. IWM

GERMAN JEWS WERE AMONG THE PARAS

Amongst the Pathfinders, there were many German Jews. Particularly motivated, the latter had received new names on their military papers, in order not to reveal their origins to the Nazis if they were captured. Two soldiers of Jewish origin had joined the 9th Parachute Battalion of the 6th Airborne. Dressed as Germans, their mission was to create confusion by deceiving the enemy with phoney orders or by turning round signposts, in a mission reminiscent of Skorzeny's SS commandos (*Einheit Steinlau*) during the Battle of the Bulge.

The battery at the Pointe du Hoc: should it be taken with paratroopers or by an amphibious assault? US Air Force

THE CHOICE OF TARGETS

The overall mission of each division being decided, they now had to proceed to the choice of targets. That was not done without ad hoc readjustments. At first, COSSAC's plan was to send in an American paratroop battalion to neutralise the threat from the battery on the Pointe du Hoc. SHAEF was worried because its 155 mm guns were capable of reaching both *Utah* and *Omaha* beaches. In the final *Neptune* plan this task was to be entrusted to a Rangers Task Force in the course of an amphibious assault.

Secure the left flank

On the 17th of February, 1944, Browning told Gale about the role his division was to play during the invasion, which was to protect the left flank of the entire operation. To do this, Gale had to capture the bridges over the Orne at Ranville and the canal at Bénouville, and destroy those across the Dives and the Divette at Bures, Robehomme and Troarn. To avoid a wide dispersal of the force over the objective, the assault on the Bénouville and Ranville bridges would use gliders. For Gale, the first priority was to establish a solid bridgehead to the east of the Orne and consolidate it against a possible German counter-attack on *Sword Beach*. For that they had to hold Ranville and the ridge a few kilometres to the east and north of the village. In addition, the 6th British Airborne was to neutralise the Merville battery to allow the landings to proceed unhindered. This was a very ambitious

The Merville battery, which threatened Sword Beach, was the objective of Lieutenant Colonel Otway's 9th Parachute Battalion. Photo Rémy Desquesnes

task to entrust to young soldiers, the majority of whom had never fought before. Neither the general staff nor the division doubted the 6th Airborne's capability of fulfilling its mission.

Support the assault on Utah Beach

As for the 101st Airborne, the plan decided on in February 1944, and later amended, set out that Taylor's men would need to support the landing at *Utah Beach* by protecting the beach exits by neutralising several enemy strongholds, and controlling the area north of Carentan to guard the bridge-head against any German counter-attack from that quarter. A large number of the 101st glider units would arrive by sea, for two reasons: 1) Leigh-Mallory advised against using too many gliders in a region of enclosed fields such as the Normandy *bocage*. 2) There were simply not enough glider pilots available.

Protect the right flank

The other American airborne division, Ridgway's 82nd US Airborne, was to be dropped in the Merderet sector with the mission of capturing bridges on the River Merderet and other areas, in particular Sainte-Mère-Église This town was the meeting-place of five roads and, in addition, was located very close to the landing zone. The aim was to protect the western flank of *Utah Beach* and to secure a good base for cutting across the Cotentin Peninsula. The 82nd US Airborne's position was considered particularly exposed. Task Force Raff (which under Colonel Raff had distinguished itself in North Africa at the head of the first American paratroop action against the enemy) should dash straight for Sainte-Mère-Église after landing at *Utah Beach*.

HOW TO FIND YOUR WAY AT NIGHT? HOW TO TELL FRIEND FROM FOE?

In case of dispersal, in addition to the passwords, the Allied paras adopted various means of re-uniting. The British 5th Parachute Brigade had different recognition signs: the 7th Battalion used hunting horns; the 12th Battalion motorcycle horns; and the 13th Battalion bicycle bells. Among the US paras, some battalions resorted to various audible signals: a bugle for the 3/506th PIR; a hunting horn for the 501st PIR; a bell for the 502nd PIR. An identifying sash was sometimes issued, worn on the left shoulder by the 2/502nd PIR or around the neck by the 3/502nd PIR. In case of need, flares were fired from Very pistols, but whistles were also used. A password was adopted: at the challenge 'Flash' the correct response was 'Thunder'. The rallying cry 'V for Victory ' was used by 6th Airborne. The 101st used the famous Landing crickets, which may also have been used by certain units of the 82nd, although that is not very likely. In fact it was the idea of an aide-de-camp of Major-General Maxwell Taylor, the latter wanting to avoid at all costs another dispersal of his men as had happened in Sicily when he was with the 82nd. These metal crickets were actually toys, and an order had

been placed with an English factory for a sufficient quantity to equip the 101st. As immortalised in 'The Longest Day', one 'click' should have been answered by two 'clicks'.

he Normandy Landings cricket, made famous in the film *The Longest Day* . NARA

PREPARATION AND TRAINING FOR THE AIRBORNE OPERATIONS

The Mediterranean experience

To ensure the success of *Overlord,* the SHAEF made a point of analysing the failings in the airborne operations carried out in North Africa (as part of *Operation Torch*), in Sicily (*Operation Husky*) and in Italy (*Operation Avalanche*). In order to benefit from his field experience, Gavin, the American who had commanded the 505th PIR in the Mediterranean, was promoted to adviser for the US airborne forces, and so joined the COSSAC staff. In October 1943, a memorandum from the British and American Combined Planning Staffs set out the advantages of a massive deployment of airborne forces to attack and seize the objectives. In addition to their operational advantages, the airborne forces represented a reserve as well as a potential threat which the enemy would be obliged to take into account.

THE INVASION STRIPES

During Overlord, to help avoid being hit by friendly fire, five easily recognisable black and white stripes were painted on the aircraft. These stripes, each about a foot wide, were painted on with more or less care shortly before the start of the operation. They decorated the wings and fuselage of every aircraft, apart from the easily recognisable heavy bombers, which operated at much higher altitude.

On the eve of D-Day, apart from the heavy bombers, all Allied aircraft were painted with alternating black and white stripes - called 'Invasion Stripes' - for ease of recognition. NARA

Avoid friendly fire; avoid dispersal

With its twin booms, the P-38 Lightning was easily recognizable: it could therefore undertake escort duty close to the armada without risk of confusion.
US Air Force

In Sicily, the anti-aircraft fire from the Allied fleet hit 40% of one regiment's transport aircraft, and half of the British airborne brigade's gliders ditched in the sea. For *Overlord*, the waves of aircraft would take a different route from that of the fleet of landing craft. In this way, for the 82nd and 101st, the air armada would reach Normandy on the west coast of the Cotentin, whereas the amphibious assault would land on the east coast. What is more, the direct fighter escort above the fleet would use the P-38 Lightning, whose distinctive twin booms left no room for any unfortunate confusion.

One critical lesson learned from these first operations was to train the isolated paras to reach their objectives, where they would rendezvous with their comrades, rather than training them to mount ambushes. Briefings would give every man full details about his unit's mission, so that he knew what part he had to play. The overly widespread dispersal of the drops over Sicily had convinced Eisenhower that they should create a Pathfinder unit (the Eureka/Rebecca system had been successfully tested during Operation Avalanche). Emphasis also had to be placed on the pilots' in-flight discipline; they should keep in formation at the altitude and airspeed ordered, despite the anti-aircraft fire through which they would have to fly. It was also noted that an airborne division is too lightly armed and lacks the vehicles needed for it to take on a role equivalent to that of an infantry division which, for example, may undertake responsibility for a larger section of the front line.

From Burma to Normandy

The operations against the Japanese were also full of lessons to be learned. Eisenhower was particularly interested by the use of gliders by General Orde Wingate's Chindits (British units trained to operate deep behind enemy lines in Burma. Their gliders transported many troops, performed reconnaissance, initiated raids and flew in supplies and equipment (including bulldozers for levelling airfields) to the rear of the Japanese army. Many wounded men who, in other circumstances, would have had to endure several days being carried through jungle, owed their salvation to an ingenious system of recovering the gliders using planes. Although Wingate died prematurely in a plane crash in March 1944,

The lessons learned from the operations carried out by Wingate's Chindits in Burma made a valuable contribution to *Overlord* . IWM

some specialists who had fought beside him in Burma later returned to England and joined SHAEF.

The Chindits' experience of using gliders (*Operation Thursday* in March 1944) made a little-known contribution to *Overlord*. IWM

STAFF ON THE DOORSTEP

While part of the 6th Airborne's HQ was based in London along with that of the 1st British Corps, a smaller staff section, headed by Gale in person, was installed farther away in a Wiltshire country house. The precautions taken to preserve the secrecy of the invasion preparations were marked by a certain excess of zeal and a lack of foresight; the windows were boarded up to keep out intruders but general staff had only one key for the door. One day the inevitable happened; the officer in charge of the precious key was late arriving, and when he arrived at the command post, he was greeted by the disapproving looks of the assembled ranks, upset at having had to wait for an hour in front of a locked door.

The training: shooting, marches, airdrops

Having assimilated the lessons of previous operations, they had to prepare the troops. Since large quantities of ammunition would not be available, the men were told: "Each shot must hit its target". The men were particularly prepared for combat, as well as for night navigation: how to stay on course, and how to find their way in total darkness? How could they remain in contact and continue to concentrate, despite the dangers? Darkness was an advantage for the lightly equipped and armed airborne forces. Their diet included a fair portion of carrots, in order to develop their night vision. They also learn how to dismantle and assemble, lubricate and grease their weapons blindfold. The training, partly conducted on Salisbury Plain, was particularly testing during the harsh winter months. The training exercises were rigorous, particularly

American paras training:
the same exercises had to be constantly repeated.
AP Photo

the marches which were particularly long (50 miles in twenty hours for the 13th Battalion of the 6th Airborne, fully equipped for combat), testing the physical endurance of soldiers who wanted to be in an élite unit. In July 1943, *Exercise Pegasus* took place. In the course of these large-scale manoeuvres, the 6th Airborne had to capture a heavily defended enemy battery, take ridges overlooking the landing beaches and delay the arrival of German reinforcements. Apart from the capture or destruction of bridges, it was therefore a realistic rehearsal of the tasks to be accomplished on D-Day. The tempo was picking up for all units - British and American - as winter approached. Each American parachute regiment carried out a field exercise and a parachute drop in December 1943.

THE 6TH AIRBORNE ENGINEERS AND 'ROMMEL'S ASPARAGUS'

The training of the 6th Airborne engineers had, among other things, to prepare them to clear airstrips for the gliders, which involved removing 'Rommel's asparagus' and all the poles from fields selected as *LZs* . For this, they simulated a field of 'Rommel's asparagus' at Bulford Fields, on Salisbury Plain. Different methods were tested and a working system was established: they exposed the base of the poles by removing the earth around it; attached plastic explosives in an inner tube and then detonated it; afterwards the debris was removed and the hole filled.

The Germans had planted 'Rommel's Asparagus' in the fields,
to guard against any airborne operations. The Allies had to find a way round this new danger.
This glider broke its wings on landing. NARA

Precision models
and inexperienced co-pilots

The glider and plane crews also had to prepare for the big day: formation flying, maintaining their heading, finding their way. Thanks to mock-ups, photos and films, the pilots had a fairly accurate mental image of the drop zones or landing zones. However, as the assault would be at night, good marking of *DZs* and *LZs* was essential. For the glider pilots, *Overlord* was their first operational night landing. Some soon had other worries when they discovered with astonishment that the co-pilot was in fact only a simple soldier with the vaguest knowledge of flying an aircraft, or even someone who had never performed a take-off or landing. The co-pilots were actually ordinary airborne soldiers, because there were not enough trained pilots to go round. In addition, although the British glider pilots had learned the tactical rudiments of infantry combat, their American counterparts had not received any such training, through lack of human and material resources within the US Army. The glider pilots also had to maintain the necessary trim of their aircraft and ensure proper load distribution within the glider (Horsa pilots could achieve this balance by using weights). Hardware had to be lashed down tightly, failing which the pilots were liable to be

A jeep is hoisted aboard a Horsa on April 22 1944, probably in the course of *Exercise Mush*. IWM

crushed by a vehicle or a gun if the securing straps broke on landing. Although glider exercises were rehearsed, after D-Day one American pilot regretted that he had been principally trained in dawn or daylight landings, both in the United States and in England. In April, the IXth US Troop Carrier Command had 2,100 Waco gliders and 300 Horsa gliders, but trained crews were available for only 951 gliders.

A new exercise:
the night jump

They moved on to jump exercises. American doctrine originally advocated a simultaneous mass drop from aircraft. The British proposal put forward was, on the contrary, that the aircraft would fly in single file and that the paras jump only as and when the aircraft reached the *DZ*. The training for a successful airdrop required a lot of work. First of all they carried out flight missions to the designated parachute drop zones. A night jump was something new for many paras. This type of training also required the greatest attention from the pilots, more often than not novices, who had to navigate their way over an England plunged into black-out. However, even when the parachutes were all ready and the containers were in place, on several occasions an exercise was cancelled due to unsuitable conditions. At other times, after the take-off, while the red light was on in the hold and the paras were waiting for the light to turn to red to signal the jump, the Jumpmaster in charge of the stick finally abandoned the jump and ordered the men to sit down again; fog had come in. It was sometimes very difficult to tell the paras that they would not be making the jump.

Airborne troops in their glider: the landing, very dangerous, required exhaustive training, IWM

A Horsa glider photographed at Brize Norton before its departure for a night exercise. IWM

TRAINING ACCIDENTS

In the course of one exercise, a British paratrooper's parachute became caught in the tail wheel of a Dakota. The hapless paratrooper was dragged behind like that for hours, having to endure the air currents and faced with the prospect of a horrible death. Finally, the aircraft flew just above the waves over Studland Bay and the strap connecting the parachute to the aircraft broke. The man did not survive the ordeal. This was not likely to demoralise the paras, as they were volunteers for this work and fully aware of the risks. On another occasion, an inflatable dinghy stowed under a wing became detached and wrapped itself around an aileron, making the aircraft uncontrollable and forcing the crew to abandon the aircraft in full flight.

The *Red Devils* in training: *Exercises Bizz* and *Mush*

On February 6th, the 3rd Parachute Brigade carried out a training jump during an exercise involving 98 aircraft.

A new milestone was reached by the British 13th Battalion during *Exercise Bizz I* when, for the first time, the pilots

Often disparaged by their parachuting comrades, the soldiers transported by gliders were not volunteers. IWM

The advantage of the Horsa is obvious in this snap: twenty-eight combatants were carried in a battle-ready group. IWM

The first training jumps were dreaded, but accidents were rare. IWM

were from the USAAF. The practices of the Americans on board the aircraft were somewhat different from those of the RAF: some crew members smoked cigars, others made coffee. The exercise took place in daylight in good weather, the C-47s, duly escorted by fighters, headed for France before turning back for the airdrop over England. On the ground, the exercise continued with the mission to capture a bridge over the River Thames near Faringdon. On this occasion, a group of volunteers led by Lieutenant Hodgson swam across the river by night. A week later, *Exercise Bizz II* involved several units of the 6th Airborne being transported aboard 284 aircraft.

Three truck-loads of airborne infantrymen simulated the arrival of gliders and declared the bridge captured on a *coup de main. Exercise Mush* was on a completely different scale. Running from the 21st to the 25th of April, it involved the two British airborne divisions, the 1st and 6th, not without causing some dissention in the ranks of the latter since they took the role of the Germans on the ground, whereas the entire 1st Division made the airdrop. General Browning was quick to ease their minds by assuring them that the 6th Airborne would make the first airborne assault on the continent. In the event, the 1st Airborne went on to meet their destiny at Arnhem, in September 1944.

Exercises Beaver and Eagle for the Screaming Eagles

The airborne Americans also carried out large-scale training exercises. Slapton Sands, near Torquay, was the ideal training area for the 4th US ID and the 101st US Airborne. The site was similar to *Utah Beach* with, importantly, a flooded area inland of the beach. The paras could therefore be trained for capturing the two narrow wooden bridges, as well as of two other passages passing through this area, represented by white bands laid out by the sappers, just as on D-Day they would have to secure the four exits from *Utah Beach*. From the 27th to the 31st of March, at Slapton Sands, *Exercise Beaver* involved a landing of the 4th US ID and elements

The Americans carried out several large-scale training operations, such as *Exercise Beaver* in March 1944.
NARA

of the 101st US Airborne, while the paratroops and glider forces arrived in trucks to the rear of the beach. During this exercise, a certain amount of confusion was noted in the transit camps, in the assembly areas and during the landing. They would have to persevere, noting the shortcomings and inadequacies, and resolving them before D-Day. The Americans drew several lessons from it, so that in April a similar exercise showed an appreciable improvement.

On May 11th and 12th, a dress rehearsal which involved the 101st Airborne was held: *Exercise Eagle*. Using the transit camps and airfields which would be used on D-Day, with a few exceptions, the entire division was dropped between Hungerford and Newbury during an exercise. The men were equipped exactly as for D-Day; the flight times were duplicated. As would be the case on that day, the Pathfinders were the first to be dropped: they had to place and operate their beacons. The purpose of the four-hour exercise was to simulate the flight times, and their arrival at the turning points and jump zones. 75% of the air-drops were accurate. Company H of the 502nd PIR was dropped in error above the village of Ramsbury when the radio operator of the leading aircraft thought that he was to switch on the Aldis lamp (which signalled the other aircraft to go to green and start the drop), whereas the pilot had simply asked him to check it. There was a

A difficult exercise: learn to drop the paratroopers without scattering them all over the area. NARA

deplorable tally of 436 injured, and 28 aircraft returned to their base without having dropped their paratroops. The arrival of the gliders went smoothly. The paras and the airborne troops launched several dawn attacks, and went on to capture all their designated objectives. *Eagle* was apparently sufficiently successful to reassure the Allied airborne forces staff: the operation would be a success. However, a very serious incident occurred on returning from the exercise. Once the pressure was off, some pilots relaxed their vigilance. The two serials (groups of aircraft) of the 316th Troop Carrier Group, each of 36 aircraft, suddenly found themselves on a collision course; as the two formations met, the pilots tried diving, climbing and swerving to avoid disaster, but two C-47s could not avoid colliding. What if that were to be repeated several times on D-Day?

D-Day is near! *Exercise Fabius I* added final refinements. IWM

Company D was the best for the operation

Each unit learned how to fulfil its assigned mission. This was especially the case for those assigned to the bold *coup de main* operations. Brigadier Kindersley assured Gale that Major Howard's D Company of the Ox and Bucks was the best unit to capture the Bénouville and Ranville bridges. To test this company's combat ability, Gale organised a three-day exercise before making his final choice. D Company had to capture three bridges defended by a small group of paras. Howard and his men impressed Gale. Audacity and quick action were the key words of this audacious *coup de main.* To evade the enemy's vigilance,

In March 1944, the 506th PIR received a visit from Churchill and Eisenhower: they had to encourage the boys!

the assault would be at night, after having closely approached the objectives with the greatest possible stealth. Howard left the meeting with pride. Even so, he did not want to leave anything to chance. If only one glider managed to reach the objective, then it would be essential that his team would comprise the elements to complete the mission. Consequently each glider carried sappers to disarm the explosive charges believed to be set on the bridges. In case the sappers were put out of action, each soldier received training in handling and neutralising explosives. If the airborne force could not take Bénouville bridge intact, the alternative was that elements of the 7th Battalion would cross the canal using thirty boats. In addition, four gliders were scheduled to land two hours later. On board they would have more boats, in particular, rafts for the anti-tank guns, equipment for the crossing and jute mats to deal with the muddy banks.

The Ox and Bucks underwent intensive training at Ilfracombe, in Devon. They especially practised urban combat in ruined English villages. At the end of those three weeks of training, Howard's men demonstrated their endurance with a march of 210 kilometres which led them back to Bulford Camp, on Salisbury Plain. One hundred and forty steps a minute: sustained momentum. Four days of marching, two in heavy rain and two in the spring heat. After arriving at camp, the officers had to inspect all their men and ensure that those who needed care were sent to the infirmary. Only then could they return to their quarters and enjoy a well-earned rest. These

Churchill and Eisenhower attending a jump exercise: the paras had to be ready so that the Allies could get a foothold on the continent. IWM

soldiers, physically strong, were turning into élite troops. Aware of the quality of their preparation, those men were confident. Howard had thus forged the perfect tool for the mission that he had been assigned.

June 5 Playing cards, under the gaze of the RAF crews. In a few hours, it would be real war, in Normandy.

A small part of Normandy in England

The repetitive exercises eventually caused boredom among some of them. Seeking to make the training ever more realistic, Howard sought out a place as similar as possible to the area around the Bénouville and Ranville bridges. There was just such a place in England, near Exeter, said George Chatterton, the Glider Pilot Regiment's commander. These bridges spanned the River Exe and the Exeter Canal, at Countess Wear. In May, as D-Day drew ever closer, Howard moved to the area, where training continued. For six days, the Ox and Bucks and the sappers were trained in capturing those two English bridges. Each exercise allowed them to refine the assault tactics, and to resolve the detailed difficulties which arose. To add to the realism, Howard required the bridge defenders to be dressed as Germans. The local residents hardly appreciated the arrival of those soldiers. It was feared that the exercises would weaken the structure of these national monuments. It was also deplorable that some soldiers used grenades for fishing - one grenade damaged the roof of a neighbouring house. During *Exercise Mush*, Howard's men had to capture a bridge over the River Thames, at Lechlade in Gloucestershire. The bridge was defended by the 1st Polish Parachute

The sea invasion forces also trained without a break: they had to reinforce the paras as quickly as possible on D-Day. IWM

Led by their officers, the men were trained in all the life-saving reflexes, and became the elite troops. IWM

Brigade. The Ox and Bucks lay down in areas marked on the ground to represent the glider landing sites. At an arranged signal, it was announced that they had 'landed'. The bridge was taken, but the referee judged that it had been destroyed by the defenders. He also said that there had been some friendly fire: a failure, then. Howard drew yet more lessons from it. To identify themselves at night, the men of different sections should simply call out the word corresponding to the alphabetical letter of their section, as they used on their radio sets. *'Able"* for A section, *'Baker'* for B section.

The training for landing the six Horsas of the *'Coup de Main Party'* had begun earlier. They had made replica landing areas for the glider pilots, at Home Camp. It was a V-shaped meadow, lined with trees similar to those planted to the south-east of Bénouville bridge, later to become Pegasus Bridge (code name *Euston I*). Another meadow, representing the one located near the Ranville Bridge (*Euston II*) was surrounded by a row of trees with flags on the other three sides. Training for the *'Coup de Main Party'* started six weeks before D-Day. To simulate the load of airborne infantrymen, the gliders carried steel as ballast. The entire flights were carried out in real time; after an hour and a half in the night sky, they had to finish with a safe landing on the two small fields. The last glider exercise took place on May 30.

A P38 Lightning prepares for take-off. The Allies' control of the skies allowed them to contemplate a large-scale airborne operation. NARA

A HIGHLY ACCURATE MOCK-UP

Howard assembled the glider pilots in a Nissen hut at Tarrant Rushton: they were surprised at the wealth of detail made known to them. A very realistic model had been built on a sand table, with everything in place: trees, ditches. The model's designer, Squadron-leader Wright of 38 Group, had had the ingenious idea of fixing wires over it, on which they could move a camera so that every pilot could watch a simulation of the final approach as seen from the cockpit of a glider. There was a quality of information, with every last detail updated following the latest reports from the Resistance, and a professionalism which had everything needed to inspire confidence.

Full-scale reconstruction for Otway

As with the preparations for the Bénouville-Ranville *'Coup de Main Party'*, the assault on the Merville battery was

The Merville battery could not be neutralised by aerial bombardment: it had to be taken by an airborne assault. IWM

meticulously prepared. On April 2 1944, Brigadier Hill told Lieutenant-Colonel Otway that his 9th Parachute Battalion would be responsible for a mission of critical importance: to take and neutralise a strongly-defended enemy battery. At the field HQ of the 6th Airborne, Otway, at first surprised to be shut in a room on his own, discovered an extremely accurate model of his objective along with a large array of aerial photographs. This profusion of details, adjusted according to the reports received, allowed him to form his plan of attack. The operation raised many problems, not least the ability of the paratroops to make their way through the Normandy countryside from the *DZ* to the rendez-vous. The taking of the Merville battery was critical, so they did not stint on the ways of refining their assault

AN UNUSUAL TEST FOR THE 9TH BATTALION

The secrecy surrounding the operation remained paramount. To test his men, Otway used an unusual ploy by sending twenty-two pretty girls from the WAAF (Womens Auxiliary Air Force) into the cafes and pubs of Newbury to see if the paras would keep mum. Otway was reassured; his men passed the difficult test without fail.

The supreme test imagined by T. Otway: resisting the charms of the female auxiliaries! IWM

Right
Parachuting dogs also took part in the liberation of Europe! IWM

preparations, as shown by a full scale replica of the German positions, built near Newbury. The search for realism in the preparation was such that each landmark, each farm, each hedge and each ditch between the battery and *DZ* V were also reproduced. Mobilising bulldozers and excavators from all over the United Kingdom (notably from Liverpool and Plymouth, where they still had ruined buildings to clear away), the site was completed in a week of working day and night. One exercise followed another, the operation becoming second nature for the men who ended up knowing every detail of the target by heart.

The plan required audacity. It also meant leaving nothing to chance. Otway considered that the success of the assault depended on landing seventy men in gliders directly into the heart of the battery. They would be commanded by Captain Gordon-Brown. All being parachutists, the idea of being landed from gliders was very disappointing because it meant that there would be no operational jump. Nevertheless, Otway did not lack volunteers for this perilous mission. They needed to be trained to fly and land these heavily-laden gliders onto a very small, narrow target. They were relying on casemates to slow down the landings by breaking off the wings! As for the former paras, their condescension toward the glider airborne troops disappeared: their greatest worry was no longer being equipped with parachutes, just in case.

PARACHUTING DOGS!

Some exercises could seem incongruous. In January 1944, Lance-Corporal Bailey, from the 13th Battalion's reconnaissance platoon, was given orders to study the possibility of parachuting military dogs. These were used particularly for messages, and some even proved able to detect mines by smell. Their acute hearing also made them good guard-dogs, able to detect the least enemy approach. Brigadier Hill carried out airdrops of dogs with the idea of entertaining his men. The mission entrusted to Bailey was considerably more serious. In April, the training of chosen dogs allowed them to consider their first jump. Everything went perfectly. So it was that a dog unit would participate in the D-Day airdrops. J. Bing, Bailey's dog, suffered eye and neck injuries on D-Day, landing in a tree where it remained suspended throughout the night. In the end, four other dogs were trained - Flash, Monty, Ranee and Bob. Two dogs, equipped with medical equipment, were also trained with the men of Otway's 9th Battalion. The 1st Canadian Parachute Battalion also had a para-dog - Johnny.

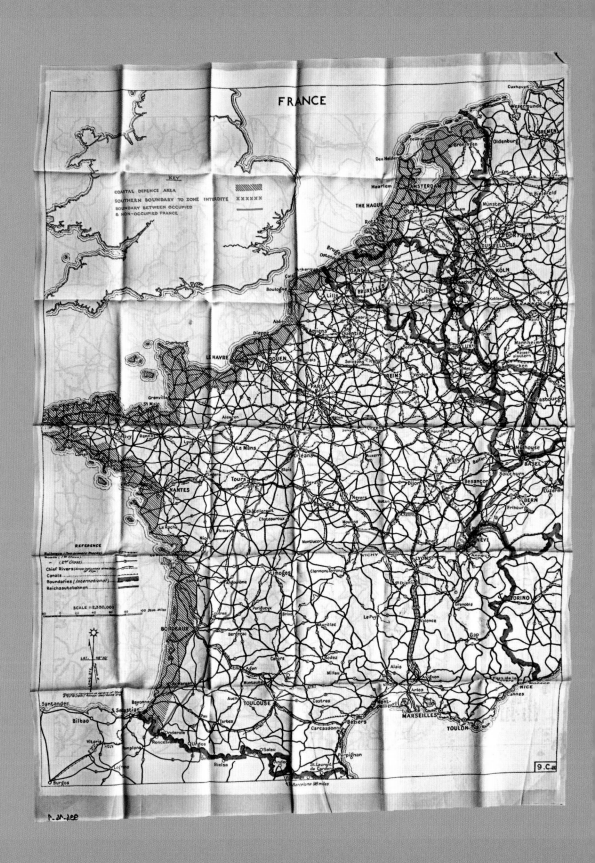

JUNE 5: THE EVE OF BATTLE

'LET'S GO!'

The paras: confined to camp as D-Day approached

In late May, the paras left their camps to go to guarded secure zones (known as 'sausages' because of their oblong shape on the map) surrounded by barbed wire, where they were briefed. They knew that the big day was approaching: the time for exercises was over. Without special permission, all leave and all contact with the outside world was strictly prohibited. Security measures were just as draconian on the airfields. A C-47 pilot remembered that he had to ask permission to go to the toilet, and an MP escorted him there from his room.

They tried to pass the time: dice, cards, football, baseball, reading, naps, writing and endless equipment checks. Sid Capon, of the 6th Airborne, found another way to pass the time. While using his binoculars, he discovered a group of scantily-dressed women's auxiliaries and enjoyed the show until a comrade burst in. They also did gymnastic exercises. The paras received the necessary equipment for orientation, such as printed maps. New weapons, such as Hawkins grenades, were issued, as were their rations. They maintained the fight-

Silk scarves, printed with detailed maps, were distributed to the paras to facilitate their escape and return to the Allied lines. NARA

ing spirit of these already highly motivated troops. Colonel Millet, commander
of the 507th PIR, ordered his men to
sharpen their parachute knives. All cold
steel weapons were sent to Nottingham,
where a local firm willingly sharpened
them without taking anything in return.
The wait during the first days of June
was in magnificent sunny weather. The
paras received combat rations and also
new forged French banknotes, actually
printed in the United States or the United
Kingdom. Any vehicles and guns not
already stowed on board were hoisted by
hand into the gliders. For the pilots, after

The paras had to help each other put on their harnesses and secure their equipment. NARA

their last dances with Englishwomen and
American nurses, the time of waiting had
also come to an end.

Final Briefing

When the officers were called to the
model and map rooms, many were aware
that they were living through a momentous
occasion, and their emotions ran high.
The operation would take place in France,
in Normandy. The officers were hearing
names previously unknown to them, but
which would go down in history. Sainte-
Mère-Église, Carentan, Bénouville. Maps,
models and aerial photographs provided all
the essential information that they needed.
After the officers, it was the turn of the other
ranks to hear the details of the operation.
Every man had to know the overall mission
assigned to his division. Wherever he found
himself, in any circumstances, he had to
make himself useful for the final success of
the landing. Leslie Cruise, of the 505th PIR
of the 82nd, learnt that he was to jump over a
peninsula named Cotentin. The young para
was amazed at what he saw; the least hedge
and the smallest river were reproduced on
the model. It was not easy to remember, and
even more difficult to pronounce, all these
names in French, a language that very few
of them spoke. They discussed the potential

Remarkably accurate models showed the objectives, with a wealth of detail. IWM

Aerial photographs (here the Longues-sur-Mer battery) proved indispensable
for the D-Day preparations.

difficulties that might have to be faced and solutions were sought. Some, like David E. Thomas, of the medical corps, were more blasé; he had been in other airdrops and knew full well that no plan was ever followed to the letter. The man was pretty casual about it all. These pre-embarkation briefings were in effect a mark of professionalism. Rarely had a military operation been prepared with such meticulous care.

D-Day postponed!

On June 4, the weather suddenly deteriorated. However, the paras had received the order to get ready. At last! The tension was beginning to become unbearable and a few fights broke out between the GIs. Canteens were topped up, pockets were filled with grenades and magazines loaded with cartridges. Then came the dreaded announcement: a twenty-four hour postponement. They then had to empty the magazines to ease the springs, and defuse the grenades. It was a tremendous disappointment; they would still have to wait. Even worse, so the rumours ran, if the storm was prolonged, the amphibious assault would go ahead without the support of the paras: an unimaginable prospect for Otis Sampson, of the 82nd Airborne. The paras had

Emergency rations were issued. This one belonged to Private Tolman, of the 6th Airborne. IWM

> **LAST MEAL**
>
> For the13th Battalion of the 6th Airborne, a hearty meal was served two hours before takeoff. "The machine gunners" wrote Lieutenant Sharples, "went off to war on two slices of bully beef, mashed potatoes and salad, followed by rice pudding with raisins." Some, like Eric Bedford, had kept back some bottles of beer, although all alcohol consumption was forbidden in the twenty-four hours before the flight.

trained for months for the invasion; they couldn't possibly be left behind. In any event, these wild rumours were unfounded. On June 4, conditions were far from ideal, but taking into consideration the advice of his chief meteorologist, Group Captain Stagg, after some hesitation, Eisenhower decided to launch the assault on June 6. On the morning of the 5th, the paras therefore repeated their preparations of the previous day.

Eve of battle

Shortly before the departure for the airfield, there was time for a religious service. Some had been to confession in the previous few days, including all the Catholics of the 501st PIR, declared their padre Francis L. Sampson proudly. On boarding the lorries (some even went by bus when there were no more lorries), the paras and the camp personnel who had

served them exchanged a last salute. The regiment's cooks lined up along the road with some of the women's auxiliaries. Many had tears in their eyes or stifled a sob. The Padre, Foy, of the machine-gun unit of the13th Battalion, noted the encouraging cheers of the villagers of Keevil as the lorries passed by. Yet for some there was to be a last minute let

The airborne troops received counterfeit French money, printed by the Allies: all set for France! IWM

Religion was a comfort to many soldiers at the time of the supreme sacrifice (here on Omaha Beach, after the battle). NARA

down. On June 5, Sergeant Buttler of the 6th Airborne, broke his shoulder playing rugby; to his great disappointment, he could not take part in the great adventure. On the airfields, the wait before the battle was still a difficult time. They tried to break the boredom on this long day, June 5 1944. The men lay down on the runways or on the apron, beside the gliders or aircraft.

While the crews were busy painting on the black and white invasion stripes, Sergeant McNiece, who had Indian blood flowing through his veins, painted his nose, cheeks and forehead with the still wet black and white paint, completing his preparations for going on the warpath. In fact he had also shaved his head, leaving only a ridge of hair over the middle of his skull, like a Mohawk Indian. His comrades in his stick from the 506th were enthusiastic and quickly imitated him. Others daubed their faces with blacking from half-burned corks or used the special tubes of green, beige or black cream.

Clarence C. Ware (left) and Charles S. Plaudo, from the 506th PIR HQ group of saboteurs, with Indian-style haircuts and warpaint, as inspired by Jake McNiece, an authentic North American Indian.
US Army Signal Corps

'Ike', anxious about the predicted losses, came to meet paras of the 502nd PIR before their departure for Normandy. NARA

IKE AND HIS GIS

Anxiety over the predicted losses within the airborne forces, and aware of his responsibilities as supreme commander, Eisenhower decided to meet the men of the 502nd shortly before their take-off for Normandy - a meeting fully in keeping with Ike's character. For their part, the paras' morale was high; the long wait was finally over. They offered reassurance for Ike, who was impressed by their confidence. He joked with his men - some of whom were more interested in his driver, Kay Summersby, a young British woman. An informal discussion took place: Ike asked his men what State they came from and enquired about their morale. Wallace C. Strobel told Ike that he was from Michigan. "Oh yes, Michigan is a great state for fishing. I have been there many times and I loved it." Later, Ike said to Kay Summersby: "It is really hard to look a soldier in the eye, when you think you are sending him to his death." On all the bases, shortly before the departure, the crews and airborne troops were given a message from their Commander-in-Chief.

The time to board had come! Some units of the airborne operations were conveyed by sea. NARA

THE EMBARKATION
The fateful moment - D-Day

A single word was contained in the sealed envelope that Major Howard received on the evening of June 5: "Cromwell", the codeword meaning that the invasion would begin that night. The order was finally given: "Embark!" No-one had time to let his mind wander; they busied themselves with the many tasks, so many times rehearsed. For a number of the British, this was the moment to enjoy a cup of tea, the drink essential to their well-being in all theatres of operations. Overloaded with materiel and equipment, some soldiers of the airborne units struggled to stand up to strap on all of their gear. Some men claimed that they had doubled their weight

Left
A British para's 'legbag'.
Coll. Tanguy Le Sant

Right
You had to get aboard the C-47 with an impressive load of kit. NARA

with their equipment (some carried boxes of grenades, each weighing 4.5 kilos). Often they needed help from their comrades. The men strapped each other into their parachutes. With all these packs, it was sometimes impossible to bend down to pick up something; one airman picked up a para's helmet from the ground to hand it to him. The men lined up by their gliders or aircraft.

Some of them decorated the fuselages with drawings or a few pertinent words; some wrote women's names, those of their wives or fiancées left at home. Reflecting on the way the Wehrmacht had found it impossible to invade England in 1940, one Horsa carried a message intended for the enemy: "The Channel stopped you, but not us." Other sentences were also addressed to the Germans: "Remember Coventry." Some outlandish requests were made: a dispatch rider approached Captain Royal Taylor of the 508th, bringing him a bicycle equipped with a parachute which Lieutenant-Colonel Warren wanted to take to Normandy. Taylor, whose plane was filled to bursting with hardware, agreed; but the bike never made it to Normandy. Taylor didn't hesitate to get rid of it.

The fuselage was decorated with chalked messages ... IWM

Military speeches

Gale's last briefing to his men before the battle. IWM

Officers addressed their men one last time at the moment of boarding. "The Hun thinks only a bloody fool will go there," said Windy Gale. "That's why I'm going!" The paras of the 6th Airborne appreciated the remark, which was greeted with cheers and applause. Brigadier Hill reminded his men that they were certainly well trained but added that "you must not be distracted if chaos reigns. It will undoubtedly reign!" They did not all have the gift of speech-making: Major Krause (3rd Battalion of the 505th PIR) seemed barely capable of anything other than oaths. However, he waved the star-spangled banner that his men had hoisted over Naples and gave them a rendez-vous at Sainte-Mère-Église, where the flag would again be flown. While some reminded their men of the importance of their mission, others invited them to pray. Major-General Taylor asked them especially not to be captured by the enemy.

At the 506th PIR, Colonel Sink reminded his men that the next day, the historic day for which they had been preparing for so long, the world would learn that the invasion had begun, and that they had to strike hard. He finished by asking God to watch over them.

"ARE YOU WITH ME?"

Jumpy Johnson, the commander of the 501st PIR, was particularly theatrical. Unable to draw the knife attached to his boot, in the course of his flamboyant speech, he took a Bowie knife, waved it above him, and swore that he would plant it in a German in France before nightfall on June 6. "Are you with me?" The assembled troops replied enthusiastically with a unanimous "YES". "Good hunting!" concluded Johnson.

An imposing force

The pilots, also briefed before boarding, were given red glasses, which were to dilate the pupils and thus improve their night vision. They were assured that they would not meet any opposition from the Luftwaffe's aircraft in the skies. As to flak, at worst it would only be a few rounds. The flight and parachute procedures were reviewed with the Jumpmasters (the NCOs of each group on board who ordered the paras to jump). In an attempt to be reassuring, they declared that the drops would be carried out as planned, in the required conditions.

The C-47 transported most of the airborne Allies during *Operation Overlord.* NARA

Landing Zone N, north of Ranville. IWM

June 5 1944. A row of Short Stirlings, which were used in *Operation Tonga*. IWM

The numbers tackled by the transport squadrons were impressive. Just counting the infantry, they had to transport 33 battalions of paras and airborne infantry (24 American, 9 Anglo-Canadian). *Operation Albany* sent up 433 C-47s carrying 6,900 men of the 101st Airborne; *Operation Boston* involved 378 C-47s with 6,400 paratroops of the 82nd Airborne on board; for *Tonga*, 5,000 soldiers of the 6th Airborne were transported in 422 aircraft and 96 gliders. Including *Operation Mallard*, the airdrops at the end of June 6, a total of 354 gliders were used by the 6th Airborne on D-Day and only ten of them were lost before reaching the landing areas. As for the Americans, 516 gliders (including 313

on June 6) were used. The D-Day total was therefore 1,233 transport aircraft and 871 gliders.

Sergeant Nibley from the101st Airborne's HQ was one of the airborne troops who missed his appointment with history. He landed by sea because his place in the glider was taken by the Division's second in command, General Pratt. More dramatically, at the Spanhoe base camp, a grenade exploded while the men of the 505th PIR were about to embark. Three paras were killed and all the others, with one exception, were wounded. The C-47's wing caught fire. The sole survivor was able to find a place in another aircraft and so participated in D-Day.

OVER THE CHANNEL

Take-off for Normandy

The roar of engines announced the imminent departure; the pilots released the brakes; the planes lined up on the runway. There was nothing more to do but wait for the signal light from the control tower to clear them for take-off. The men were sitting more or less comfortably, waiting for the flight, each lost in his own thoughts, according to his character. They're off! Strapped in their

Below
The armada en route for Normandy: an unforgettable sight for the airborne troops, who could see it. NARA

This colour photo, taken on April 22, 1944 during an exercise, shows a stick of Red Devils, with one of them wearing the famous maroon beret. The system of hooking up the parachute harness can be clearly seen. IWM

cockpits, the pilots began the take-off procedures. The rhythm was impressive. All types of aircraft were covering the aircraft parking areas and tarmac of dozens of airfields. The take-off: a plane took off every ten seconds, so that it needed only a few minutes for an entire squadron to take off. The imposing Allied air armada took to the sky. At 22:30, the first of the six Halifaxes from 298 and 644 Squadrons, towing Major Howard's men, took off from Tarrant Rushton. At the airfields, all the off-duty personnel watched the spectacle, not without lumps in their throats. The emotion was intense.

When visibility allowed, on board the gliders or aircraft, the airborne troops saw the astonishing and comforting sight of the incredible Allied naval armada; a multitude of dark shapes leaving a white wake on the waves, filling the sea as far as the eye could see. In the C-47s, the roar of the engines was so loud that the men were unable to talk to each other most of the time. They thought about the battle to come, their families and their loved ones. On board the gliders, the pilots had to use all their skill to hold the correct attitude in relation to the towing aircraft. In the holds, more than one airborne soldier suffered from nausea and soon vomit spread over the floor.

At sea level

The planes were flying at low altitude (150 meters). No radio contact was allowed. No lighting either, except for a few small blue lanterns. In the American group, they increased altitude to 450 meters to avoid the Channel Islands and their flak before dropping down to 180 meters. Approaching the *DZ*, the flight engineer in the leading plane took his place in the plexiglass turret and sent a light signal to the other two aircraft in their V formation, to tell them to go from red to green, the jump signal. The pilots were under strict orders; no para was to be returned to England unless either he was injured or an equipment malfunction prevented him from jumping. Those who refused to jump faced court martial.

View of the inside of the cockpit of a Horsa glider. IWM

The Channel crossing took place in scattered clouds and calm weather. Boats with beacons - the vessel code-named Hoboken was stationed north-west of the Channel Isles - helped them to follow the correct course. Arriving over Normandy, the pilots were faced with heavy cloud formations. "Flying in near-zero visibility", wrote General Gavin, "virtually wing-tip to wing-tip, the pilots quickly had to decide how to save their crew, their paratroops and their aircraft." The pilots were afraid of collisions: they spread out, climbed, or descended even lower. So low that some paras, like John Taylor, joked: "No need for a parachute for this! We are so low that a rope ladder would do".

Over the objective; ready to jump!

American paras of the 101st, with blackened faces. NARA

They stared at the Jumpmaster, who communicated by gestures. The men stood up when they saw him raise his arm, then fixed their hooks to the static line when he made a hook movement. It was a safety measure: better to hook on in advance, in case the aircraft was hit and they needed to make an emergency jump. They then had to check their equipment, and that of their comrade standing in front them. When the Jumpmaster put his hands over his ears: each parachutist slapped the arm of the man in front, yelling a reassuring: "OK!" Ready for the big jump: the tension peaked. These young men sweated, vomited and prayed, but they were ready to fight.

The fateful hour, for which there had been so much preparation, had come: the paras were confident and ready to go. DR

AHEAD OF THE PATHFINDERS: ON D-DAY - 3

Around 01:30 on June 3 1944, the vanguard of *Operation Overlord* took the form of a few teams of daring commandos and members of the secret services who came under the OSS (Office of Strategic Services), the American espionage service. Each team was composed of two American soldiers and three British commandos of the SAS (the Special Air Service, a commando unit). Their mission was to prepare for the parachuting of the Pathfinders in order that the latter could mark the *DZs* in the correct place: an almost suicidal mission.

The fuselage of an Albemarle was very uncomfortable for these British paras! NARA

THE FRENCH SAS IN BRITTANY

During the night of June 5 - 6, the first paratroops dropped as part of *Operation Overlord* were in fact French, of the 3rd and 4th SAS. Between 00:30 and 00:45, these men parachuted into Morbihan and Côtes-du-Nord with the mission of harassing the German units and slow their going into action.. The enemy was to be led to believe in a possible landing in Brittany. Some Jedburgh teams (from the Special Executive HQ, SOE) were responsible for co-ordinating and strengthening the local resistance, which was also given significant quantities of weapons and equipment. These few paras were only the vanguard of the SAS, who were dropped in Brittany in the days that followed.

OPERATION TITANIC

Featured in the film *The Longest Day*, this consisted of dropping 500 decoy paratroops. These were actually dummies made of canvas (Rupert) or olive green rubber (Oscar) although in the event the latter were not used operationally. These dummies were fitted with a device which caused explosions which simulated gunfire when they landed. *Titanic I* used 200 decoys, preceded by a few SAS, in the Yvetot region. Their aim was to ensure that the enemy would keep its reserves north of the Seine. *Titanic II* was an airdrop of 50 dummies near Dives, just to the east of the 6th Airborne's *DZ*. *Titanic III* was a parachute drop of 50 decoys. In the American sector, 200 Ruperts were dropped over Marigny as part of *Operation Titanic IV*. Two other SAS teams were dropped between Rouen and Le Havre, and near Isigny, carrying with them a gramophone with records on which were recorded the sounds of fighting and the screams of soldiers.

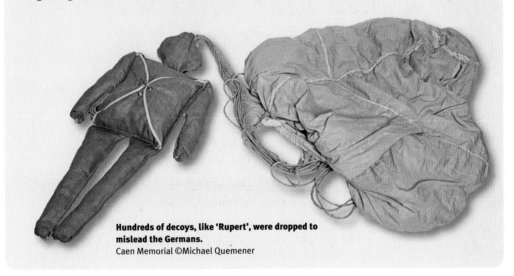

Hundreds of decoys, like 'Rupert', were dropped to mislead the Germans.
Caen Memorial ©Michael Quemener

All the men were now concentrating on the red light. They should have jumped at 150 km/h but some aircraft opened up to 250 km/h. On board the gliders, once the towlines from the towing aircraft were released, the airborne troops quickly became aware of the imminence of their landing. In the British gliders, the co-pilot shouted "Brace! *Brace!*" They then prepared to land.

The Allies had the advantage of surprise, the cover of darkness, an exceptional concentration of forces, intensive training, thorough preparation; even the weather was on their side. Would *Operation Neptune* go according to plan?

THE 101ST US AIRBORNE DIVISION SCREAMING EAGLES IN SUPPORT OF THE LANDING ON UTAH BEACH

PARACHUTING INTO HELL

"*Geronimo!*"

The pilots, themselves very nervous, noticed that the paras, usually rather boisterous, were now very quiet. General Taylor managed to get some sleep, lying on the floor in the hold of his C-47. He removed his harness and rested his head comfortably on some cushions. Shortly after 01:00, the airdrops begin. The C-47s were to drop the paras of the 101st on *DZs* A (502nd PIR), C (506th PIR) and D (501st PIR).

The formations - flying very low, at an altitude of around 150 metres - were greeted by concentrated flak and machine-gun fire: the shells and tracer bullets flashed across a black sky lit up with explosions; here and there, the yellow and orange glare reflected back from the clouds. Some aircraft were burning after being hit. Bursts of machine gun fire or 20mm shells ripped through severely damaged cockpits, wreaking havoc

Pathfinders Stick No. 5 of the 101st: a difficult, but essential task awaited them. NARA

PATHFINDERS IN DIFFICULTY

Captain Frank Lillyman, leader of the 101st's Pathfinders, was the first American para to jump, cigar in mouth, and to hit the ground in Normandy on this historic night. Captain Taylor's C-47 had a forced landing in the sea. Although all the men survived, thanks to their Mae Wests, and were able to hoist themselves into a life raft, the *DZ* for the 506th would not therefore be marked. Only the Pathfinder teams assigned to *DZ* C (101st) and *DZ* O (82nd) were dropped close to their objective.

Lieutenant Bobuck (3/506th PIR) inspected his men one last time. NARA

and destruction. The firing was so intensive that it illuminated the insides of the cockpits. Some pilots of the stricken aircraft managed to keep their planes flying long enough to allow the paras to jump, thus sacrificing their lives for their comrades of the airborne forces. They had to jump: *"Geronimo!"* was the war cry of the 501st PIR.

Griffing, one of the paras of the 501st PIR, saw and heard 20mm tracer rounds flying past him. He instinctively curled up, feeling that his end was near. Fortunately for him, the appearance of another serial of C-47s diverted the attention of the flak gun crews who had been aiming at him: saved! Once landed on the ground, more than one para was isolated. McClung, of the 506th PIR, landed near Sainte-Mère-Église. He met a soldier named Payne of the 501st PIR, with whom he joined the 505th PIR (82nd Airborne) for around nine days.

SAVED BY AN OLD INDIAN RUSE

Some paras owed their survival only to their own good sense and their rapid reaction to danger. Spreading chaos in the chateau of the Haut Fornel, Lieutenant Smit and Private Boone suddenly found themselves trapped in front of a wall that they could not climb. Only one way out: hide underwater in the pond. Remembering some westerns seen in the cinema just before D-Day, Smit breathed under water through the barrel, removed from his M3 tommy gun!

Boarding: the moment of truth is near! NARA

Some less than discreet crickets

Some of the aircraft finally returned to England with their paras; the pilots had not lit the green light. For two other aircraft, the airdrop ended in tragedy when the paras jumped over the Channel. In yet another incident, the Jumpmaster, Colt 45 in hand, forced the pilot to go back Arriving on the ground, the paras of the 101st used their crickets. Were they that discreet? Not exactly, if we are to believe the testimony of one of the *Fallschirmjäger*, Oberjager Griesser: "If they had croaked like frogs, nobody would have noticed in the marshes, but the noise of these steel clickers was so unnatural that you would need to be deaf not to notice." Some landed far from their *DZ*, as did four paratroops of the 506th PIR, landing at the foot of the Pointe du Hoc cliffs. Two of them joined in the assault by the Rangers led by Lieutenant-Colonel Rudder.

Flak, far from being neutralised, was daunting for the C-47 formations. Bundesarchiv

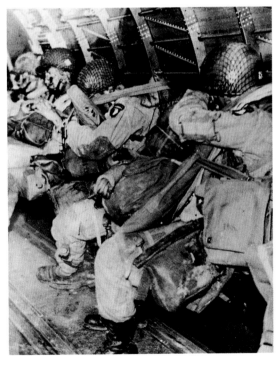

Men of the 501st PIR HQ. The paras were met by a hail of fire. NARA

TO CARENTAN

Objective achieved at La Barquette

The capture or destruction of the bridges on the Douve, to the north of Carentan, was the mission for a group from the 501st and 506th PIR. 1,475 paras of the 501st (the first two battalions) had to capture the lock at La Barquette, and two bridges on the N13. Lieutenant-Colonel Carroll's 1st Battalion of the 501st PIR was too widely dispersed to complete its mission, Carroll having been killed, so the commander of the 501st PIR, Colonel Johnson - known as Skeets - decided to capture the La Barquette lock. Johnson jumped late, the door to his Dakota being blocked by a case of K rations; a useful delay which allowed him to land closer to the objective. As he marched towards the objective, he watched the terrible sight of a mid-air collision between two C-47s, which burst into flames before immediately crashing into the ground. Little by little, he managed to assemble one hundred and fifty men of his own 501st PIR and other units. Arriving at the lock, the paras found it undefended: not one shot was fired. A small bridgehead was established on the right bank of the river.

Two other bridges were the objectives of the 3rd Battalion of the 506th, called to assemble by a bugle, who had to pass

The bridge at the La Barquette lock: the D-Day objective for Johnson's 501st. DR

Two paras of the 101st inspect a house on the edge of the Carentan marsh. NARA

The Allied forces engineers had several bridges available, but it was essential to seize
the existing structures, and prevent the Germans from using them. NARA

the Douve and establish a bridgehead near Brévands, pending the arrival of the troops landing further east, on *Omaha Beach*. Meanwhile, at the port, Captain Shettle (with only about fifty men instead of a battalion) reached the wooden foot bridge and road bridge built by the Germans in 1943, but he could go no further. Fast running low on ammunition, he had made preparations for the destruction of the bridges, just in case. As for Johnson, he kept two hundred and fifty men with him at La Barquette where, so far, no threat had appeared.

Johnson gets irate

A little further east, in Saint-Côme-du-Mont, one of the objectives of the 2/501st PIR, led by Lieutenant-Colonel Ballard - who had suffered the unpleasant experience of crawling through nettles - the paras were faced with the *Fallschirmjäger*, and it took them several days to win control of the area. Having his hands full dealing with the enemy, especially at Angoville-au-Plain and Les Droueries, Ballard was unable to capture Saint-Côme-du-Mont and so could not go to the rescue of his superior, Colonel Johnson, who believed that his subordinate had abandoned him. At 08:00 hours, after two and a half hours of combat at Les Droueries, German machine guns and mortars had caused the loss of one third of his force. Ballard then mounted a flank attack with one company while engaging the enemy from the front. The Germans were tenacious: their defence line did not give way. Another attempt on the right flank, through the marshes, also failed. That evening, a little before 22:00 hours, Ballard, short of ammunition, had to send some men to the *DZ* to find fresh supplies.

NEUTRALISING THE COASTAL BATTERIES

D-Day begins for Cole:
a rosebush and a battery already destroyed

How to assemble the men? There are the crickets. But they sometimes created such a racket that it became impossible to distinguish the calls from the answers: who made that click? Where? For whom was it meant? Towards 04:00, Lieutenant-Colonel Cole (commander of the 3rd Battalion of the 502nd PIR), had gathered around him only one hundred and twenty men, and was preparing to attack the battery of Saint-Martin-de-Varreville (one of the objectives of both Colonel Moseley's 502nd PIR and Lieutenant-Colonel Chappuis' 2nd Battalion), when Captain

Gliders on the *Elmira* or *Keokuk Missions* flying over Utah Beach in the evening of June 6. DR

Lillyman reported that the battery had been bombed into silence several days before. No guns had been left on the site, apart from one gun destroyed when the bunker had collapsed (a similar misfortune occurred at Pointe du Hoc, unnecessarily attacked by the Rangers, since the Allied intelligence services had not been aware that the guns had been withdrawn). Cole had suffered a violent landing, falling into a rosebush. He had also encountered some difficulties of orientation as he had arrived close to Sainte-Mère-Église by chance, without however trying to capture it, as it was not his mission. In addition to helping Chappuis, who had injured his leg when he landed, to destroy the enemy battery, Cole's other mission was to secure two exits from *Utah Beach*. He went on to try to complete his mission with a mixture of paras from the 502nd, 505th, 506th, and 508th.

Summers' exploit

The other battalion of the 502nd, the 1st, commanded by Lieutenant-Colonel Cassidy, had to neutralise a complex known as XYZ. By chance Cassidy had met the injured Lieutenant-Colonel Strayer (2nd Bn/ 506th PIR): together they had a force of two hundred paras, and Cassidy went forwards again toward his objective. He then met Captain Lillyman, with whom he left a few men to set up a road block. One of Cassidy's GIs was about to perform a real exploit. Dropped near Saint-Martin-de-Varreville, Staff Sergeant Summers had with him only a mixed bunch of paras from different units, who were not used to fighting together. These men were reluctant to take part in the attack against objective W, less than

Ravenoville, June 6. The paras got their hands on a French half-track, reused by the Wehrmacht. DR

Saint-Martin-de-Varreville: it was essential to secure the exits from Utah Beach. NARA

2 kilometres from Mésières. The Staff Sergeant decided to first neutralise a complex of eleven farm buildings serving as billets for anti-aircraft gunners (objective XYZ). Summers decided to lead by example, seizing the first building on his own. He had already neutralised thirty-one Germans when, arriving at building 9 and assisted by Private Camien, he surprised fifteen other Germans sitting eating at a table. They were astonished that these soldiers of the Wehrmacht could act so casually while airdrops were taking place and the fighting had begun. Seven paras were killed, however, and four others wounded during the course of a charge across open ground

during the fighting for the last two buildings. Staff Sergeant Nickrent approached in his turn, and sent several bazooka shells into the first floor and the roof, putting to flight more than eighty Germans who had to run to escape exploding ammunition and who, caught in the cross-fire, were massacred, with fifty killed. In total, one hundred and fifty Germans were killed or taken prisoner. "I wouldn't do that again in the same circumstances," said Summers. Courage? Sense of duty? Still, thanks to the perseverance and the training of the élite paras, the men of the 101st proved themselves formidable opponents against the Germans.

Sainte-Marie-du-Mont

Taking Sainte-Marie-du-Mont was one of the 506th PIR's missions. The forces of Lieutenant-Colonel Ballard and Major Allen failed to take control of this small village. They were confronted with a formidable opponent: the *Fallschirmjäger* of the FJR 6. Captain Patch, at the head of a mixed group of 506th and 502nd, took the Holdy battery with its four 105mm guns - a battery unknown to the intelligence services. Leaving the guns in the care of the paras of the 502nd, Patch continued his advance from Holdy to Sainte-Marie-du-Mont: one of these guns was used by Sergeant King to provide covering fire. Unfortunately, a shell hit the bell tower of the church where a dozen American paras had sought shelter during the night (which contradicts Heydte's claim to have seen the Allied fleet from the top of this bell tower). These paras fired on some Germans crossing the square, but when they saw an American tank, fearing to be hit by friendly fire, they waved the Stars

Sergeant George Vercey at the entrance to the church in Sainte-Marie-du-Mont. A few paras spent the night in the steeple, concealed from the eyes of the Germans. DR

and Stripes. Although the tank held its fire, that was not the case of the crew of the captured gun. Meanwhile the Germans held the rest of the village. It was a fierce fight, and the GIs opponents, the *Fallschirmjäger*, did not retreat until tanks from *Utah Beach* arrived.

GIs waiting to wash their mess tins under the fascinated gaze of Norman children. NARA

WAR CRIMES

The Holdy sector was the scene of several tragedies that took place that night near the German battery. Some paras suspended in trees were massacred, others were found with their genitalia cut off, and some paras of the 502nd were burned, sometimes alive, draped in their parachutes after having been stabbed or bayoneted.

CONTROLLING THE EXITS

The control of Exits 1 and 2 fell to the 506th PIR under Colonel Sink (which had been dropped with elements of the 326th Engineers). The 502nd PIR and paras of the 326th Engineers had to keep Exits 3 and 4 open. Around 01:15, parts of the 501st and 506th PIR were dropped north of Hiesville. A few seconds delay in jumping was sometimes enough to end up isolated: Sergeant Rogers, of the 101st, thus lost precious time pushing a mortar cart out of the door of his C-47. How to find your way at night? Shots and screams shattered the silence but these hedges, paths and houses definitely all looked the same. They asked the French, not always sure about the identity of the person they were talking to. Some, like Corporal Louis Merlano, were dropped by mistake on the dunes, in the middle of the Atlantic Wall defences. Others, like Major Lawrence Legre, owed their survival to their own presence of mind. Stopped by a German patrol, Legre replied in French, explaining that he had just been keeping his girlfriend company, and that he was sorry to have missed the curfew. While speaking, he drew the pin on a grenade that he threw at the German patrol, killing all three.

Paras of the 502nd and 506th PIR at Marmion farm in Ravenoville: sticks of all the units, scattered to the four winds, were mixed up during the airdrops. DR

HOW DO YOU GET OUT OF A SWAMP?

Jack Womer fell into a marsh. In training, he had been taught that any trees in sight would indicate the way out of a marsh. Thanks to his cricket, he found another para and they went in search of a way out of the flooded area. At that moment, a plane exploded, illuminating the whole sector for thirty seconds. That was enough for Womer to see some trees, and so find his way out of their predicament.

Band of Brothers at Brécourt

Like the other GIs, Lieutenant Winters and Sergeant Lipton, of the 506th PIR, tried to discover where they were: where had they landed? A signpost soon showed them that they were in the suburbs of Sainte-Mère-Église. The plane carrying the company HQ Staff stick, hit repeatedly, crashed into a hedge where it blew apart in an explosion. Winters did not yet know it, but he was the acting leader of Easy Company of the 506th PIR. For the time being, he had to set out for their objective, near Sainte-Marie-du-Mont. The Germans had accurately identified the best areas for an airdrop of paras or landing gliders. On these particular sites they had astutely sited machine-gun nests so that entire fields were covered in their field of fire. At Brécourt, the farm was deliberately set on fire to illuminate the area, so making it easy to spot targets falling from the sky.

Men of the 506th's renowned Easy Company, made famous by the series *Band of Brothers*. DR

It had been established that there was a 105mm battery close to Brécourt, and Lieutenant Winters was ordered to wipe it out, since these guns effectively had Exit 2 in their sights. This episode has been immortalised in the Band of Brothers series. Winters led the attack with ten men, organised into two groups:

Flak: many transport aircraft and gliders were damaged or totally destroyed in the course of the operation. NARA

The effects of a bombardment by the Boeing B-17 Flying Fortresses were terrifying. The USAAF however mistakenly destroyed a bridge over the Douve canal, previously seized intact by American paratroops. NARA

Lieutenant Compton's group would deal with the first gun, with covering fire from the second group, led by Winters in person. Supported by bursts from two 30 mm machine-guns, Compton attacked the maze of trenches around the battery, which was located in a field enclosed by hedges. Reinforced by some GIs from HQ, the paras disabled the guns with explosives. The charge by D Company inspired by Lieutenant Speirs reduced the German's fighting spirit to nothingness, and they fled without further ado. Mission accomplished.

Billy Green, a para of the 506th, did not make the big jump on D-Day: flak puncturing the floor of his C-47 caused his parachute to open prematurely; it then inflated under the effect of the air currents, filling part of the hold.. Nevertheless his comrades were able to push him aside so that they could jump. Another aircraft exploded in mid-air with

its Bangalore torpedoes, instantly killing the seventeen paras on board. G Company of the 506th were to experience a major disappointment that day. Without a means of communication, they were unable to report that they had taken a bridge on the Douve. Lieutenant Doughty, who had taken the bridge, was subjected to an attack by the USAAF who bombed and destroyed the bridge. This mishap was not an isolated tragedy. The 506th also had to destroy all the bridges crossing the Douve Canal, with the exception of the largest, which had to be seized intact. McNiece managed to capture that largest bridge and, after being cut off for three days, was down to about forty men. Explosive charges had been brought with them, in case the Germans Panzers tried to force their way across. Unfortunately, once again, the USAAF bombed and destroyed the bridge, causing the death of fifteen American paras in this action.

Exits 1 and 2
were controlled

At the start of D-Day, Major-General Taylor was in the same straits as many of his men: he was alone. When, at a bend in a hedge, he finally met another paratrooper, the two men were so happy that they fell into one another's arms. He then found Brigadier-General McAuliffe (the future hero of Bastogne), about forty paras led by Lieutenant-Colonel Ewell, and then a group of his staff. Taylor mustered altogether about one hundred men; he should have had 1,200 with him. In this small group they counted no less than two generals, two colonels, one major, several captains and eight lieutenants. Taylor later paraphrased Churchill with the comment: "Never in the annals of war have we seen so few men commanded by so many officers." He led them towards Pouppeville and Exit 1, which should have been taken by Strayer's 2nd Bn/ 506th, and where Turner's 1st Bn / 506th, sent by Sink, were pinned down. The Americans finally won control at the end of the engagement with soldiers of the 91 Luftlande-Division. Towards midday, contact was established with the troops landed on *Utah Beach.*

The airborne force and the 4th US ID joined forces at Exit 2, which was held under the control of men from Lieutenant-Colonel Strayer's 2nd Bn/ 506th. Strayer had fortunately benefited from a relatively close-grouped parachute drop; but on the wrong *DZ* (he had met Cassidy to the north of the parachute zone, whereas he should have been to the south). The latter, having managed to assemble two hundred and twenty men by 03:30, then had to make the entire journey on foot with them, finally arriving at the objective, Pouppeville and Houdienville. They were met with fierce resistance at Saint-Germain-de-Varreville, and it was only at 13:30 that they reached Houdienville, which was taken without a fight.

GIs of the 4th US ID paddling through the water covering a track above the beach: without the paras' support, it would have been difficult to progress inland. NARA

The odyssey of Colonel Sink's jeep

Paras aboard a Kübelwagen captured in Carentan, which was not taken until June 11, after fierce fighting. Colonel Sink very nearly lost his life on board the American equivalent: the famous jeep. NARA

Colonel Sink, worried to be still without news of his 3rd battalion, left to search for them in a jeep, along with two other men. Suddenly, his vehicle burst out on to a road where a German company was taking a few moments of rest. The GIs opened fire as they drove the jeep at them, forcing the Germans to take cover until Sink, realising the attack was too risky, ordered the driver to turn back. By some miracle, no American was injured and no German bullet hit the jeep. The 3rd battalion that Sink was looking for was very much dispersed. His commander, Lieutenant-Colonel Wolverton, was dead and the four company commanders were missing.

Exits 3 and 4 - an easy success for Cole

The mission entrusted to the 502nd PIR - the control of Exits 3 and 4 - was proving to be less difficult. The first paras jumped over *DZ* A shortly before 01:00 hours. Cole who, it will be recalled, had arrived in error at Sainte-Mère-Église after having witnessed the destruction of the battery at Saint-Martin-de-Varreville, headed east. Shortly after 04:00 hours, after a skirmish with the Germans and with barely eighty paras, he took Exit 4 without a fight and then took Exit 3 towards 07:30. The Landing had then been in progress for one hour. Suddenly, a group of German soldiers came back up the road from the beach. Opening fire at the very last minute, the paras decimated their opponents, leaving them no chance of escape. The GIs, having suffered no losses, counted seventy-five enemy bodies. By the end of the day, Cole had mustered two hundred and fifty men of his battalion. Ordered to Blosville for the night, they were assigned to divisional reserve.

THE NORTH FLANK

To the north, the fighting went on in several small areas, to secure the safety of the left flank of *Utah Beach*. Lieutenant Muir captured Ravenoville, where ten Germans were killed and thirty others taken prisoner, thanks particularly to the energetic action of Private Brinninstool. Lieutenant-Colonel Cassidy (502nd PIR) established roadblocks at Foucarville and Beuzeville-au-Plain. In this way, a few of Cassidy's men (fifteen paras led by Lieutenant Hoggard), accompanied by Lillyman's intrepid Pathfinders, established a roadblock south of Foucarville. Hoggard, unable to take the village, received a first reinforcement

General Maxwell Taylor found himself isolated after his parachute jump. He finally managed to join a group in which officers were particularly numerous!

The parachute was fixed to the static line just prior to the Norman night jumps: they had to be ready to go, before the landings at dawn. AP Photo/Army Signal Corps

Landings were difficult: this Horsa finished its trip by crashing through a wall around the field on which it had landed. DR

of twenty-five men. He then launched a second assault but was again repulsed. At 10:30, forty-four other paras, commanded by Lieutenant Swanson, arrived in their turn. They quickly set up four roadblocks at all the approaches to the village. The day was a series of fights against those Germans leaving the coastal zone, and those from the stronghold built to the north of the village. In the middle of the afternoon, twelve paras sent to establish a new roadblock to the west of the village, ambushed a convoy of five German trucks. But the paras were quickly faced with a barrage of fire and Swanson had no reinforcements to send them. Towards 22:00, the latter was surprised to note that the Germans in a position north of the village suddenly ceased fire. He then saw some of them, accompanied by a woman, coming down from the hill, hands in the air, carrying a white flag. Others tried to flee and some were taken prisoner by the paras. In a matter of minutes, the Americans took eighty-seven prisoners and killed fifty Germans. Although all these battles were admittedly small scale, they caused significant enemy losses. By the end of the day, contact had been established with the 4th US ID.

OPERATIONS CHICAGO AND KEOKUK

The death of a General

Returning to England after dropping the paras over Normandy, many C-47 crews had to prepare for a new mission: towing gliders, most probably for the operations at the close of day on June 6. A few repairs were carried out and they re-filled their fuel tanks. The pilots, feeling nervous after their first experience, knew that they had to go back there. The first C-47 of *Operation Chicago* took off at 01:19, the plane being flown by Colonel Whitacre. It was towing Lieutenant-Colonel Murphy's glider Fighting Falcon, on board of which was General Donald Pratt, second in command of the 101st. According to the version of events given, Pratt was sitting either in his jeep or next to Murphy, which would have meant that there was no co-pilot, on a seat specially reinforced underneath with armour plating. Unlike the aircraft which had transported the paratroops, the aircraft towing the gliders approached the Normandy coast from the east, flying over *Utah Beach*. Just a few seconds after reaching the shore, the cables were released. The lights from the lamps of the *LZ* E (for East) could be seen. However, the full moon was of limited use because of the scattered clouds which dotted the Normandy sky. In addition, the pilots became more nervous upon seeing the dark silhouettes of the trees along the hedgerows. The landing area was completely flat; the fields which made up the area stretched for 250 to 300 metres. However, they were surrounded with hedges with trees sometimes over 30 metres high - much higher than the small hedges which the pilots had seen in England. This was a disconcerting surprise. From his cockpit, Emile Natalle saw with some concern the warm reception which awaited him - gunfire, explosions, vehicles in flames. Many landings were extremely hard: Natalle's Waco broke in two, just behind the jeep, but, he thought ironically, that would make it easier to offload

Paras of the 1st British Airborne Division embarked for Arnhem in September 1944: that time, the airdrop took place during the day. IWM

Horsa gliders proved particularly fragile: the Americans stopped using them. DR

Chicago was relatively successful: the damage inflicted by the Germans was minimal. One pilot went off course, and released his glider south of Carentan, but only six gliders reached the landing zone. The relatively light loss of only twenty-eight men (including four killed) was regrettable, but significant given that they had yet to tackle the Germans. As for their equipment, it took them some time to unload it from the gliders, because of the sporadic German fire. Guns were particularly needed - six anti-tank guns had been brought in by one detachment - since, in the night, the 377th Parachute Field Battalion's drop went wrong, so that the 101st had only one 75mm Pack Howitzer, near Foucarville, as well as a captured German gun, sited close to the 506th's PC at Culoville.

the vehicle. Murphy's glider reached the field at an excessive speed and crashed into a hedge at more than 150 km/h. Pratt, having climbed aboard the glider in England did not survive the crash.

The jeeps arrived by glider: the paras gained mobility, but the German resistance was fierce. Carentan (here) did not fall on D- Day. DR

The 52 Waco gliders of *Operation Chicago* carried Batteries A and B of the Airborne Anti-aircraft Battalion, as well as medics, engineers, HQ staff and signallers: a total of 259 men including the pilots; sixteen 57mm anti-tank guns; 25 jeeps; one bulldozer; 2.5 tons of ammunition; and 11 tons of other equipment. They lacked the 101st HQ's SCR-499 radio, which was in a glider which had broken its cable on taking off back in England. It only arrived at the end of that day, June 6 as part of *Operation Keokuk*.

The *Keokuk Mission* involved thirty-two gliders and as many aircraft: reinforcements for the 101st arrive!

D-Day's last reinforcements

There was a wait of 21 hours before the gliders of a new airborne operation - Operation Keokuk - brought reinforcements for the *Screaming Eagles*. The landing path was clearly indicated by yellow signs and green smoke in the form of a 'T'. Flying over *Utah Beach,* their exposure to flak was by then minimal. The mission consisted of 32 Horsa gliders carrying 221 men, 6 guns, 40 vehicles and 19 tons of equipment. The Germans, who had held back from firing at the Dakotas, seemed to concentrate on the Horsas, but this gunfire, at extreme range, had very little effect; the gliders arrived at the *LZ* in very good visibility. Even so, fifty-four men were lost (including fourteen killed): one quarter of the troops on board.

On the evening of 6th of June, they had joined up with elements of the 4th US ID who had landed on *Utah Beach*, but many paras were still missing, and they did not know how strong the enemy reaction would be in the following days. By midnight, barely 2,500 men were directly under the command of Maxwell Taylor and his HQ.

This superb line-up of Halifaxes, Horsas and Hamilcars photographed at Tarrant Rushton, awaiting departure with the 6th Airlanding Brigade (6th Airborne) bound for Normandy. It symbolises the power of the airborne Allies in this fifth year of the war. IWM

THE 82ND US AIRBORNE DIVISION ALL AMERICANS : SECURING A BRIDGEHEAD ON THE MERDERET

THE DISPERSAL OF THE AIRDROPS

Jumping in a sky criss-crossed with tracer

The Dakota squadrons were ferrying the paras of the 82nd to *DZ* N (508th PIR), T (507th PIR) and O (505th PIR). As with the 101st, the 82nd's pathfinders had not been able to complete their role, and so the airdrops were widely scattered due to the many over-cautious pilots, often novices. Unlike the aircraft carrying the 101st, the C-47s with the paras of the 82nd on board decided to cope with the cloud cover by flying above it. Although that protected them from flak, their landmarks could not

This famous photograph of Lieutenant Kelso C. Horne, taken after D-Day, illustrates the need not to be distinguished from subordinates when facing the danger of snipers: a Garand rifle, like the troops, and no visible marks of rank. NARA

Pathfinders Stick 3 of the 508th PIR, 82nd Airborne. Notice the jumping smocks,
carefully camouflaged by the paras themselves. DR

be seen. Many aircraft were flying far too high, at an altitude of 700 metres, which put the paras in danger since it increased both their dispersal and the time taken in the descent under enemy fire. The first airdrops took place towards 01:51, nearly an hour after 101st airdrop had started, and under fire from the now well-prepared anti-aircraft guns.

Standing in their C-47s, the paras of the 82nd waited for the red light to change to green. Some were yelling with impatience. Then, at last, the jump into enemy-held territory under the withering fire of German automatic weapons; a terrifying experience. "The chute tightened in my crotch, as the planes droned overhead," recounted Leslie Cruise (505th PIR), "and I knew that my chute had opened though I could hardly look up to see it. I had suddenly slowed as the chute fully opened and I floated in space, as I began my more leisurely descent. Leisure is not the best word as tracers whistled by, and I began to hear them again as I never heard before." A man who had parachuted did

Supplies, materials and equipment were also parachuted in by C-47s. IWM

A group of paras making careful progress in Saint-Marcouf. DR

not stay long in the air, generally between twenty and thirty seconds. He dropped quickly and the ground approached fast. Concealed by the darkness, the parachutist did not make an easy target. The paras had other fears - trees, high voltage power lines, flooded areas and waterways where, despite wearing a Mae West, it was easy to be drowned under the weight of all the equipment. The dispersion was widespread. Having landed in the swamps, General Gavin, with a handful of men, did not at first know where he was, until they discovered the Caen - Cherbourg railway track reassured him of their location. Paddling around in the water, his priority was to save the containers and their contents - bazookas, mortars, radios and other equipment - which the men would desperately need. All around, even though lost, the paras had every intention of completing their mission. To achieve this, the first priority was to reach their rallying points as quickly as possible. The orders were clear: they should not burden themselves with prisoners, who would only slow down their progress and be difficult to guard. Every man counted.

NO PRISONERS!

More than one prisoner was shot after his capture, in flagrant violation of the Geneva Convention. Many Airborne Americans would be taken prisoner that night, whereas others were gunned down in cold blood. Lieutenant Goldsmith (of the 505th PIR), along with a few other paras, was quickly disarmed while they were still caught up in their harnesses. Not wanting to be encumbered by prisoners, nor to attract attention by opening fire, the Germans who had just overcome them satisfied themselves by breaking their hands with their rifle butts before locking them in a barn.

SAINTE-MÈRE-ÉGLISE

Two paras suspended from the bell tower

The airdrop of Colonel Ekman's 505th PIR proved to be the most successful of that historic night. Even so, their reception was terrifying. Flak was flying from every direction. The explosions shook them. Instinctively, the men curled up on themselves. They would have to jump into this hell! The tocsin was ringing in the town of Sainte-Mère-Église: a house was on fire, probably started accidentally. While the inhabitants braved the curfew and attempted to bring the fire, which was being spread by the wind, under control, a few stragglers of the 101st Airborne were shot dead by the German garrison. Ray Aeibischer, of the 506th PIR, escaped by a miracle and managed to get away safe and sound. At 01:40, more clusters of parachutes appeared above the small town. Ken Russell, of the 501st, was at the forefront of the tragedy that was played out at Sainte-Mère-Église: "When we arrived, we could see a building on fire. The flames were visible for several kilometres around.

General Theodore Roosevelt Jr, commander of the 4th US ID, at Sainte-Mère-Église: the first town to be liberated by the Americans was taken by the 82nd, during the night. NARA

A para charges towards the church of Sainte-Mère-Église. A few Germans were quartered in the steeple, but the scene is probably reconstructed. NARA

A parachute still hangs from the church roof in Sainte-Mère-Église, in memory of John Steele. In fact, two paras found themselves hanging from the church, but they were on the front, opposite the square ... Antoine Pascal

The pilot had dropped us over the centre of Sainte-Mère-Église: it was terrifying; most of the guys from our stick stayed there. Some never set foot on the ground. As I floated down, I saw on my right a comrade disappear in a blinding flash; he had been carrying a Gammon grenade on his hip. All that was left was his parachute, which continued to fall on its own. The intense heat of the fire drew the nylon parachutes like a magnet. I heard John Holsbeck shout once, then a second time, just before he landed on the burning house; and then I heard nothing more." Russell himself landed on the church, his suspension lines caught on the bell tower, on the opposite side from the square. He saw another para, John Steele, also suspended from the holy edifice, who has since gone down in history thanks to the film, The Longest Day. Steele, captured and injured in the foot, remained deaf for several weeks because of the continuous ringing of the bells.

Several Americans were shot in the town centre: at least three were left hanging from telephone poles, like hanged criminals. A para had just reached the first floor of a house, where a shot was fired in his direction; he shot his attacker, a German soldier's French girlfriend. Other paratroops landed in the gardens of the surrounding houses and managed to slip away into the night.

The GIs take the town

At 4 o'clock in the morning, one hundred and fifty men of the 3rd Battalion of the 505th PIR, led by Major Cannonball Krause, finally took control of the crossroads at Sainte-Mère-Église Krause thus successfully completed his D-Day mission. The task was hardly difficult since the village was defended only by about fifty Germans, the majority of whom were captured after a skirmish. Krause had ordered his men to enter the area with their weapons empty and to use grenades and cold steel, aiming to avoid friendly fire incidents. Any shots would give away the Germans' positions. The town thus became the first French mainland town

A reconstructed scene of hunting out snipers at Sainte-Mère-Église. DR

to be liberated by the Americans. Later, in the early morning, and after several orders and counter-orders, since Ekman didn't know that Krause had seized the important crossroads, the 2nd Battalion of the 505th arrived on the scene, led by Lieutenant-Colonel Vandervoort, who had broken his ankle during the jump. Vandervoort, who was sitting in a folding trailer (he changed to a jeep later), mustered 400 men out of the 630 (this rose to 575 by the evening of June 6).

First German counterattacks

To the north of the town, this same 2nd Battalion set up a roadblock at Neuville-au-Plain: Vandervoort thus reinforced the few men to whom Ekman had assigned positions. Some elements of Krause's battalion were also called upon. Forty-one paras commanded by Lieutenant Turnbull were assigned to this critically important mission. At first having only a single bazooka and a solitary machine gun, they were strengthened later when they received a 57mm anti-tank gun. The courage and tenacity of this handful of GIs repulsed several counter-attacks, repeatedly mounted throughout the day, by Major Moch's Battalion of Infanterie-Regiment 1058 of the 91. Luftlande-Division. This battalion attacked from the north, supported by nine Sturmgeschützen and

an anti-aircraft company, as well as some armoured personnel carriers from the Panzer-Abteilung 100, a rag, tag and bobtail unit who had only some ancient captured French tanks and a single Panzer III, by then obsolete. But these armoured

FAILURES OF THE MEDICAL SERVICE

Corporal Moore of the 3rd Battalion, 508th PIR, was seriously wounded and begged to be allowed to die. There was neither morphine nor plasma. Like the rest of the paras' equipment, a significant part of the Division's medical equipment had been lost, who knew where.

vehicles could still prove dangerous for the paratroopers, who had very few heavy weapons. The whole unit was not lacking strength. The advance, along the high hedges of the region, was determined and the assault was carried out with artillery support. The first attack was launched at 10:30. Private Cruise, of the 505th PIR, testified: "We had roadblocks set up on all the roads leading out of Sainte-Mère-Église, and in the adjacent fields troopers from the third battalion were covering their flanks from foxholes dug during the night and early morning." German artillery and mortars were making life difficult for the defenders. A para, Vargas, at the same position as Cruise, was seriously wounded by a mortar. But the paras had learned first aid and they had all been issued with first aid kits. While the firing continued, Cruise, although nearly fainting after discovering his comrade's multiple puncture wounds, fought to save his life, making up a tourniquet from a belt,

The 42nd US Field Hospital in Sainte-Mère-Église. Injured Germans wait to be treated beside wounded Americans. NARA

giving him a morphine injection and calling for a medic. Turnbull held his road block for more than six hours, suffering twenty-five losses. This resistance allowed Krause and Vandervoort to concentrate their efforts on repelling another threat which had materialised from the south.

The Germans did not give in

At 09:30, the Ost-Bataillon 795, supported by five armoured vehicles, attacked Krause's roadblock. Krause, come to see the situation for himself, was wounded in the right leg by a piece of shrapnel. The situation was critical, so two companies and a 57mm gun were engaged to repel the enemy. Krause sent Captain Swingler and eighty-four men to outflank the German positions from the west, but the company failed three times, Swingler himself being

fatally wounded. However, the Ost-Bataillon 795 withdrew to Fauville. From the east, infantry of the Sturmabteilung AOK 7 and some armoured vehicles of the Panzerjäger-Abteilung 709 made an unsuccessful attack from Beuzeville-au-Plain. These disjointed counter-attacks lacked coordination and, more particularly, scale. By the end of the day, the American losses at Sainte-Mère-Église were forty-four dead and one hundred and thirty wounded.

THE BRIDGES AT LA FIÈRE AND CHEF-DU-PONT

Isolated on Hill 30

In addition to capturing Sainte-Mère-Église, the 505th PIR had to secure the bridges at La Fière and Chef-du-Pont. The La Fière bridge was the objective of Colonel Millet's 507th PIR, who were to take the western end, and Colonel Ekman's 505th PIR who were to secure the eastern side, at Le Manoir de La Fière, comprising a handful of houses, stone bridge and a long drive. The La Fière and Chef-du-Pont bridges also involved the 508th PIR under Colonel Lindquist (they also had to seize the bridges over the Douve at Brienville and at Beuzeville-la-Bastille). The mission began under a cloud since the major part of its two thousand paras missed *DZ* N.

Lieutenant-Colonel Shanley, who commanded the 2nd Battalion, 508th PIR, only assembled three hundred men, to the west of the Merderet. Nevertheless he decided to head for the objective. Blocked by a group of Germans, he made the mistake of thinking that he could not reach the bridge and so turned back towards the east. On the way, he amalgamated his force with two hundred men who were with Major Warren of the 1st Battalion, and two hundred other paras who were awaiting developments. He fell back to Hill 30, which he discovered was of little military value. In addition, the position was very precarious; the hill was surrounded by the enemy on three sides, and the fourth side was blocked by the Merderet marshes. Lindquist, who had managed to make contact with Shanley, promised him reinforcements for the next day.

Ceremony for feats of arms which took place during D-Day with decorations awarded by General Bradley at the Château of Broqueboeuf, near La-Haye-du-Puits. The man with the cane is Lieutenant-Colonel Vandervoot (John Wayne in *The Longest Day*). DR

Three para regiments for one bridge

A Renault half-track, destroyed at Neuville-au-Plain. At La Fière, the GIs had to face captured French tanks.
NARA

Who, therefore, would try to take the La Fière bridge? This illustrates the imbroglio in which the two American Airborne Divisions found themselves, with a mixture of units, as a result of inaccurate airdrops. Lieutenant Dolan, with 90% of his A Company of the 505th PIR, headed for the bridge from *DZ O*. Dolan, arriving in the vicinity of his objective, sent a patrol to assess the enemy Germans, of which there were only twenty-eight, in fact). Visibility was still bad, so nothing was discovered. Dolan did not immediately realise it, but little by little other American paras had arrived in reinforcement: Colonel Ekman in person, along with elements of the 505th; Colonel Lindquist with paras of his 508th; and Captain Schwartzwalder, with forty-five paras of the 507th. Dolan, ignoring the arrival of reinforcements, attacked the bridge, but the handful of Germans defenders held on tenaciously. Machine gun fire swept the terrain. The Americans, unable to use

their mortars for fear of hitting their own troops, were in an impasse, pinned down by enemy gunfire. Advancing towards the sound of artillery fire, Lindquist and Schwartzwalder, who had joined forces, were approaching the bridge from the east (Schwartzwalder had intended to go on to Amfreville, his own objective): they arrived at Le Manoir de La Fière at the same time as the paras of the 505th PIR and Colonel Ekman. The defenders at the bridge were holding on as tenaciously as ever; four of a five-man para patrol were killed. Snipers, perched high up in the trees, were a constant threat. It was then that B Company of the 508th received the order to finish off the Germans and to mount a flank attack, via the river and the marshes. In vain. At 9 o'clock another character entered the scene: General Gavin, commander of the 82nd Airborne, who arrived with three hundred paras of the 507th, with Lieutenant-Colonels Malloney and Ostberg. They assure him that the 505th would soon master the situation. Gavin, who commanded this regiment, was confident of it. At Le Manoir, after an American bazooka round and the massed fire of all the paras of the 505th, 507th and 508th deployed close by, the Germans finally raised the white flag. One GI was shot when he went forward to accept the surrender (probably from a different German position) and it took a whole new fusillade to force the defenders to surrender. The east end of the La Fière bridge was held by the American paras.

More difficulties at Chef-du-Pont

Arriving at Chef-du-Pont at 10 o'clock (am), Lieutenant-Colonel Ostberg sent a patrol through the village towards the bridge. This invasion of American paras provoked a fusillade and a desperate fight broke out, lasting for two hours, the GIs trying unsuccessfully to reach the bridge before the Germans. Two American officers, one of whom was Ostberg, reached the bridge, but were wounded: all attempts to storm the little architectural gem resulted in failure. Even worse, Lieutenant-Colonel Maloney had to retreat with his one hundred and forty men to La Fière, leaving Chef-du-Pont to thirty-four men led by Captain Creek (with one mortar, but quickly reinforced by the landing of a Waco with a 57mm anti-tank gun on board). "Hold on at any cost!" ordered Gavin.

Overconfident paras

For the Americans at La Fière, things were hardly going their way. Towards 13:45, Schwartzwalder (507th PIR) ordered Lieutenant Marr to take his section to the other side of the bridge. Marr promptly carried out this order; they now had only to follow the roadway up to Cauquigny During this time, to the west, twenty men of the 507th, led by Lieutenant-Colonel Timmes, were moving

Chaplain Sampson of the 501st PIR prayed for his comrades, fallen under fire. The losses were heavy within the two American airborne divisions. NARA

towards Amfreville where fighting could be heard. Timmes sent a patrol, which reached the roadway where it was joined by Schwartzwalder's company coming from La Fière: Cauquigny could be taken and the roadway controlled. But Schwartzwalder made the mistake of leaving only nine men at Cauquigny and went to look for his superior, Timmes, taking eighty paras with him. Meanwhile, at La Fière, they strengthened the bridge defences by laying mines, building a barrier using a wrecked German lorry, and setting up a 57mm gun. With the arrival of reinforcements, the American position now seemed impregnable.

However, the Germans were far from giving up. Indeed, at 16:00 hours, shots were heard coming from Cauquigny; a group of paras from the 508th came running up, reporting that the Germans were approaching with three armoured vehicles. The Germans were cynically using about fifteen American paras as human shields, as well as ordering them to dig up the mines as they went. Towards 17:30, the German column arrived close to La Fière bridge and a desperate fight took place along the roadway. Three tanks, formerly French tanks which had been captured, were set on fire, but the single American 57mm anti-tank gun was also destroyed. The noise of the battle was terrible: artillery fire, mortars, small arms fire and machine gun bursts spread death through the ranks of both sides. The Americans held on; the German attack was repelled. By the end of the day, the American losses at La Fière were twenty dead and one hundred and fifty wounded.

Cheese and bottles

Leaving Maloney and the men of the 507th with the 505th, who were defending La Fière, Gavin then returned to Chef-du-Pont with the paras of the 508th and 101st hoping, in vain, to find any way across the river, even by using makeshift rafts. Arriving at the Chef-du-Pont station, they surprised a train on the point of leaving; the German soldiers on board opened fire on the GIs before they left. Gavin's booty: an anti-aircraft gun, some Normandy cheeses and crates of empty bottles ...

James Gavin, decorated by Bernard Montgomery in Germany. On June 6, Gavin was still only second in command to Ridgway in the 82nd US Airborne, before succeeding him. IWM

BEYOND THE MERDERET
Drownings and dispersion

The 507th and 508th PIR drops were a catastrophe. The two regiments' missions were, respectively, to seize bridges over the Merderet and establish defensive positions to the west of the river. But the airdrops were so scattered that too many soldiers landed west of the Merderet or in the flooded areas, whereas they needed to have large numbers of troops on the banks of the river.

Corporal Schlegel had a narrow escape. His C-47 was hit in the port engine and so he rushed to make his jump: he had barely leapt into the void when the Skytrain exploded. In the sky filled with shots, including one from an enemy gunner who seemed to have singled them out, some had the presence of mind to play dead. Others were less fortunate and drowned in the Merderet marshes. How many? We will probably never know. Some sources state that thirty-six from the 82nd drowned, but there is no way to be certain. Thomas Porcella very nearly lost his life there. "I had the shock of my life. I dropped into the water. When my feet touched the bottom, I gave a strong kick to resurface and take a breath of air. The water was almost over my nose. Standing on tip-toe, I got my breath back. My heart was beating so rapidly that I thought it would burst. I prayed to God, 'Lord, don't let me drown!' I plunged back under water trying to undo the parachute straps that were wrapped round my legs." He then took out his knife to cut the straps: this was his last chance; it didn't work. Porcella started to panic, but then calmed down as he realised that he was using the back of the blade. After ridding himself of his parachute, his helmet and his explosive-laden pack, he was at last out of danger. In contrast, Lee Milkovis, of the 508th PIR landed ingloriously on a cow pat. He would reek throughout the day, much to the dismay of some of his companions. At the first opportunity, he washed his uniform.

Ralph de Weese, of the 508th, had the fright of his life. He landed in a metre of water, and had the greatest difficulty in undoing his harness while his parachute, blown by the wind, dragged him for hundreds of metres. He owed his salvation to the dagger strapped to his right ankle.

"No guts?"

Many men found themselves alone, some having lost their equipment when their straps were cut by fire. Other lost the contents of overloaded pockets, which did not withstand the shock of the parachute opening. They wandered around, sometimes for hours, in a maze of greenery, plunged into darkness. For some, the long wait, coupled with the stress of the jump, were more than they could endure: they remained prostrate, unable to move. Fatigue also weighed on these desperate men. Under fire from a machine gun, 1st Lieutenant Millsap charged towards a hedge but, despite his orders, none of his men, all lying on the ground, followed him. "What's the problem?" he yelled, "No guts?" But nothing happened. Millsap needed the help of another officer to stir his men into action. 1st Lieutenant Smith, another lost soldier from the same 508th PIR, after crossing hedge after hedge, could find only one other fellow countryman, a Sergeant; but he belonged to another unit. The two paras walked towards the sound of the guns. It was only that evening that Smith found his regiment. By then, his new-found companion had been killed. Over the hours, the noise of fighting became clearer. Then, little by little, toward the coast, the paras could make out the noise from operations on the shore; the Landings had begun!

The German command cut off

Though scattered, these airdrops made the Germans feel insecure. They do not know where the attackers were, and the slightest noise or movement in the night might have meant the arrival of the enemy. The American paras pulled off a great coup that night, during an ambush along a road. Faced with the escalating events, Wilhelm Falley, commander of the 91 Luftlande-Division, who had gone to Brittany for a *Kriegspiel* at Rennes, was in his staff car heading back to his HQ at Château Haut, near Picauville. The General's driver suddenly saw an American soldier, who burst onto the road in front of him. "Stop!" shouted the para. The driver accelerated past the American, but the vehicle was by then riddled with bullets and crashed into a farm wall. Falley crawled on the ground towards his pistol, which had

General Falley, commander of the 91st. Luftlande-Division was the victim of an ambush by the paras during the night of June 5-6, 1944.

been thrown clear, shouting: "Don't kill me, don't kill me!" He was shot in the head by 1st Lieutenant Malcolm Brannen of the 508th: the first German general to be killed during the Battle of Normandy.

THE DETROIT AND ELMIRA MISSIONS

Detroit: the first American gliders

The fifty-two gliders of the 82nd in *Operation Detroit* took off towards 01:30, about ten minutes after those of the 101st. A Waco broke its cable at take-off. The towing aircraft, however took it in tow again and, incredibly, it landed in Normandy only half an hour

A jeep trailer of the 82nd hoisted on board a Waco: gliders were indispensable for taking heavy equipment to the airborne troops. NARA

The Detroit Mission involved 220 men (326 counting the pilots), sixteen 57mm anti-tank guns, twenty-two jeeps, five trailers and ten tons of equipment.

late. The gliders of the 101st were having a much more difficult time in their mission as the flak had become much more accurate: one C-47 was shot down and thirteen others, heavily damaged, required lengthy repairs. Many gliders were also hit. The pilots were having difficulties finding their fields and orientating themselves. Some were aghast at the simultaneous arrival of so many planes and gliders. There were only thirty-seven gliders left, arriving close to *LZ* W (W for West) between 04:01 and 04:10. Twenty-two of the fifty-two gliders were destroyed and twenty others heavily damaged, much of it caused by 'Rommel's asparagus' or the flooded areas. One Waco even crashed into a herd of cows. The losses were minimal: twenty-six men were lost (three killed), and eleven jeeps were unusable. The paras rushed to retrieve the awaited guns. Near Sainte-Mère-Église, they went as far as destroying a orchard's stone wall to recover an anti-tank gun. Elsewhere, they put all their energy into recuperating another 57mm gun stuck in a Waco which had crashed, wrapping itself around a tree.

American airborne troops: unlike the paras, the infantry soldiers transported by gliders wore the same uniform as general infantrymen. NARA

Elmira - the LZ under fire from the Germans

At the end of the day, *Operation Elmira* received a new and more substantial glider landing. Suddenly, as the first tugs with their gliders arrived, all hell broke loose. But it was mostly small arms fire, and did only moderate damage. By this time, *LZ* W should have been easy to spot, but not all the markings were in the right place; in addition, some pilots confused it with the *LZ* E. Worse was to come: the situation at *LZ* W was by then very dangerous. All those who knew that would have recommended

The first phase of *Elmira* used 176 gliders towed by C-47s. To avoid congestion at the landing site and to allow a more effective fighter escort, the group was split into two, arriving with a two hour interval between them. The first group was made up of 54 Horsas and 22 Wacos. On board: 437 men, thirteen 57mm guns, 64 vehicles and 24 tons of equipment.

American glider pilots: many were inexperienced and, unlike their British counterparts, had had no combat training. NARA

landing elsewhere, as the Germans effectively controlled the northern perimeter of the fields. Task Force Raff had twice tried, in vain, to push the Germans out of this zone and the troops defending Sainte-Mère-Église were themselves cut off from the *LZ* by these enemy troops. Ridgway tried unsuccessfully to warn the IXth Troop Carrier Command; his radio message was not received, and the pilots did not see the signs that his men had laid out on the ground. Raff and his men tried every way they could to warn the approaching glider pilots, waving yellow flags and setting out the letter 'F' with orange smoke flares on the ground.

The paras anxiously awaited the arrival of the gliders bringing the heavy equipment they desperately needed. But the Germans were waiting, and the Wacos were literally riddled with bullets. The Germans were not the only danger: the area was partly flooded and they had to avoid the hedgerows and trees,

some of which were very tall. A jeep was unloaded from the wreckage of its glider, only to finish up a few metres further, blown up by an American mine laid there earlier by the paratroops. A para tried to drag a GI from of his glider by pulling his legs, but without success. Looking inside the Waco, he found to his horror that the chest of the unfortunate man had been crushed by a jeep, whose mounting straps had probably broken during the crash. The Horsa landing gear would pierce the floor of the hold when they hit the ground. Raff, an eye witness to the carnage, observed that the English-designed gliders had an unfortunate tendency to break into pieces. However, contemporary photos showed that some Horsas made a perfect landing. A glider which inadvertently landed in a mine field disappeared in an explosion. Quite a few gliders bucked on landing, collided with 'Rommel's asparagus', ran head-on into hedges or piled into other gliders in the crowded landing fields. Men were seriously injured or died impaled

The second wave of the *Elmira Mission* included 100 gliders (86 Horsas and 14 Wacos), split into two groups. The first serial transported 418 men, 31 jeeps, twelve 75 mm howitzers, 26 tons of ammunition and 25 tons of equipment. The second serial transported 319 men, 28 jeeps, twelve 75 mm howitzers, 33 tons of ammunition and 23 tons of supplies.

Landing on a Landing Zone was a consummate art: enemy fire, hedges and trees had to be avoided, as well as other gliders moving in a congested sky. NARA

on broken shafts of wood from the air-frames. There were forty-nine casualties (ten killed). Three Wacos and twenty-one Horsas were destroyed.

The initial flight plan for the C-47s of Elmira's second phase projected a 180⁰ turn to the left after the drop over the objective. Before take-off, the pilots were told that they should do the opposite, turning to the right, probably because Saint-Côme-du-Mont was still in German hands. The Eureka beacons at *LZ* O were the only ones functioning. The flak was very intense - three C-47s crashed into the sea - but there were very few deaths. The landings took place between 22:55 and 23:05, some at speeds of 180km/h under intense German fire. Fifty-six Horsas and eight Wacos were totally destroyed. Sergeant Sampson (E/505th PIR) claimed that one Waco had landed in the upper branches of a tree: "like a bird coming home to roost." There were eight losses on landing, of which 38 were killed. The men preferred to hide until nightfall before unloading the equipment. Surprisingly, the equipment was relatively spared, considering the number of gliders destroyed. The Americans were able to recover 15 out of the 24 howitzers, 42 of the 59 jeeps and 28 trailers out of 39. About 1,800 men of the 82nd arrived by glider (including the glider pilots); 226 were lost to crashes on landing. Nineteen of the 111 jeeps were destroyed as well as four of the seventeen antitank guns.

By the evening of the 'Longest Day', many men were missing. 75% had not been dropped in the right place. For most, contact had not been established with the forces landed on *Utah*. Some of the isolated units were west of the Merderet and the situation at Sainte-Mère-Église remained precarious, as did the situation at the Merderet bridges. The following days would be decisive; 2,000 soldiers of the 82nd alone were directly under the command of the general staff.

THE 6TH BRITISH AIRBORNE

THE RED DEVILS : PROTECT THE EASTERN FLANK OF THE INVASION

PEGASUS BRIDGE

Will Howard hold on?

After the *Coup de Main*, Howard decided to leave only a single section at the Ranville bridge, a sector where the paratroops of the 7th Battalion were due to arrive. Another section, along with its HQ, took position east of the Bénouville bridge. The other three sections withdrew to the west of the bridge, a critical area which had to be held against the German counter-attacks, which would not be long in coming. The anti-tank weapons were indispensable, but they noted with dismay that all but one of the Piats had been damaged on landing. During

this time, despite the dangers, Lieutenant Bence, of the Royal Engineers, examined the two bridges. Having made his calculations, he estimated their capacity at 30 tons, which would allow Sherman tanks to cross.

Toward 2 o'clock in the morning, the characteristic clanking of Panzer tracks was heard. Lieutenant Fox, in the front line at the crossroads on the road leading to Le Port, entrusted the sole PIAT to Thornton. The first German tank was hit and caught fire. The following multiple explosions confused the Germans, who thought they

Aerial view of Pegasus Bridge on the Orne canal. The three Horsas from Howard's Coup de Main party are clearly visible to the left. IWM

Inspecting the tunnels and trench shelters which the Germans had dug near the Bénouville bridge, Fox and Thornton were amazed to discover some enemy soldiers sleeping there!

were probably facing a solid position, well provided with antitank guns. They stopped advancing and missed the chance to defeat an opponent who seemed within their capacities. On the other bridge, at Ranville, Lieutenant Sweeney ambushed two light German vehicles moving along the road, with their passengers unaware of the danger.

After Major Howard's men, the first to arrive in Normandy were the Pathfinders and the advanced groups of the 5th and 3rd Parachute Brigades. The sixty Pathfinders (aboard six Albemarles) jumped at *DZ* N, V and K. Unfortunately, two of the sixteen Albermarles of the 3rd Brigade's Advance Party were hit, and six men, jumping prematurely, disappeared into the waves of the English Channel.

Two British paras dug in under German roadsigns: they had to be ready to repel the inevitable German counterattacks. IWM

Rescue of the Ox and Bucks

After a silent approach and a wild ride over the ground beside the canal, Major Howard's Ox and Bucks scrambled out of their three Horsa gliders. IWM

At 00:50, the men of Brigadier Poett's 5th Brigade, transported in 91 Stirlings, were dropped over *DZ* N, close to Ranville. It was relatively easy to identify because of the proximity of the Orne and its Canal. The HQ of the 6th Airborne was transported by forty aircraft. One hundred and thirty-one planes dropped more than 2,026 men and 702 containers. However, they were widely scattered. At the end of two hours, only 60 per cent of the paras had reached their rendezvous areas. An airdrop sometimes has some very strange events, when men are left suspended in tall trees: one para, who could not be rescued using ladders,

Horsa Bridge: the bridge which straddles the Orne at Ranville was captured, unopposed, by Major Howard's men. IWM

A half-track bren carrier crossing Pegasus Bridge on June 8. The 6th Airborne's success allowed a bridgehead to be established east of the Orne, as a flank-guard of the landing zone. IWM

had to wait twelve hours before being lowered with ropes.

Lieutenant-Colonel Pine-Coffin's 7th Battalion was airlifted to France aboard 33 Stirlings. The dropping of the remainder of the unit took place under difficult and perilous conditions: the enemy was alert and they had to jump under fire. These airdrops were also very scattered, mostly because of the cloud cover. Once on the ground, it was frustrating, Pine-Coffin realised, to know that the *DZ* and the rallying point were close, but at the same time not to know in which direction to go. The leader of the 7th Battalion's luck was in, because a flare lit up the easily recognisable bell tower at Ranville. It took a lot of time to assemble his men, assisted in this task by Lieutenant Rogers' torch and, especially, by Private Chambers who sounded the

rallying call on his bugle. By 02:15, he had still mustered only 40% of the Brigade: it was better than nothing. Furthermore, the news from Howard was reassuring; the bridges had been taken intact. Abandoning their river-crossing equipment, Pine-Coffin's *Red Devils*, were quick to rally the Ox and Bucks who were isolated around Pegasus Bridge. They joined Howard towards

Also parachuted into *DZ* N, Captain Lockey of the 591st Parachute Squadron Royal Engineers had to make contact with the sappers arriving in Howard's gliders. On arrival at Bénouville, Lockey was surprised to see that there were no demolition charges to be removed from under the bridges.

The engineers' Bailey bridges added to the ways the British crossed rivers
(here, Winston bridge in Caen). IWM

03:00 hours in the defence of Bénou-ville and its surroundings. To do this, they had barely two hundred men – too few if the enemy launched a determined counter-attack. Even worse, the special-ists, the mortar and machine-gun crews, radio operators and others, were unable to get their hands on their hardware, lost over Normandy after being dropped from the Stirlings' bomb bays. For anti-tank defence, they had only a few PIATs as well as a German 50mm anti-tank gun in emplacements near Pegasus Bridge. Wally Parr kept up a continuous fire on the enemy with this gun, to the annoy-ance of his comrades due to the incom-ing retaliatory mortar fire that his own shots provoked.

Phlegmatic under sniper fire

The sporadic sniping made for an uncomfortable situation. One round from a PIAT (or from an armoured vehi-cle) silenced those hiding in the church bell tower. Realising that the water tower would make an ideal observation post for the snipers, Parr put two armour-pierc-ing shells into the tower, raising a cheer from the Ox and Bucks when water cas-caded out. Around 09:00 hours, protected by a row of trees planted between the two bridges, three individuals seemed to pay hardly any attention to the snipers: Gen-eral Gale, Brigadier Poett and Kindersley walked quietly to meet Howard. Shortly afterwards, two small German boats, one

Just before 10:00 hours, a Focke-Wulf 190 fighter-bomber performed a brilliant feat of aviation. Avoiding the vigilance of the omnipresent Allied air forces, he reached the bridge and dropped his single bomb, hitting his target, the canal bridge. Unfortunately for the Germans, the detonator was defective and, instead of exploding, the bomb bounced into the canal and disappeared in the water.

A Sherman of the 13th/18th Hussars in a field of gliders near Ranville. The paras were not heavily armed enough to fight alone for long: they had to be reinforced by the contingents landed on Sword Beach. IWM

coming down the canal from Caen and the other coming from Ouistreham, were easily driven off by the defenders. A shot from a PIAT forced one to ground on the river bank, while the other was forced to turn back by 50mm rounds.

"Sorry, we are two and a half minutes late!"

From 07.00 hours, the noise of the shelling of the German coastal defences at *Sword Beach* by the Allied fleet and aircraft was music to the ears of the paras dug in around Pegasus Bridge; the Landings were in progress, they were no longer alone. They had to wait many long hours to hear, finally at 13:00 hours, the skirl of Bill Millin's bagpipes in the distance. Certainly, the Scottish tradition explains the fact that an officer goes into battle to the sound of the pipes. But did it not also provide a sure way of alerting the airborne troops that their relief was on the way? Millin played 'Blue Bonnets over the Border.' A bugler, reported Sweeney, responded with a call. At 13:30, Lord Lovat, supported by a single armoured vehicle, finally reached Bénouville with his commandos. But the bulk of the landing force was still far behind. For the moment, however, they felt a great relief.

Lord Lovat (in the second row, on the right) and his piper Bill Millin (in the front row) landed on Sword Beach: they had to win through to Bénouville as quickly as possible. IWM

The mission was accomplished. "John", declared Lovat to Howard, "we are making history today." Howard apologised for the inconvenience caused by the German snipers, who obliged the commandos to cross Pegasus Bridge at the double. Millin took no notice and boldly crossed the bridge with his back ram-rod straight, playing the 'March of the Camerons'. Arrived on the right bank of the Orne after having crossed the Ranville bridge, Lovat said the now famous words

Bill Millin, the legendary piper of Pegasus Bridge, playing his bagpipes for the men of N° 45 Royal Marines Commando on June 3 1944.IWM IWM

"Sorry, we are two and a half minutes late." Relaxed British humour: Lovat was actually half an hour behind schedule. In fact, it appears that these words were not uttered by Lovat, but by a Captain of No. 6 Commando, as evidenced by that unit's War Diary. Ahead of Lovat, a section of that same No. 6 Commando commanded by Captain Pyman, had reached Bénouville towards noon, one hour before Lord Lovat! However, Pyman had himself been preceded by others: the first units landed by sea had reached Bénouville even earlier in the morning, at around 11:30; sappers of 1629 Assault Platoon, part of the 106th bridging company, Royal Army Service Corps, had in fact received orders to advance rapidly on Bénouville to begin the construction of two Bailey bridges in case the *Coup de Main Party* had not succeeded.

Glider N° 91, carrying Major Howard as well as Lieutenant Brotheridge, who fell on the bridge at the start of the assault. Only the intensive training insisted on by Howard gave such precision in the landings. IWM

On the evening of June 6, reinforcements also arrived by air, such as these gliders photographed near Ranville: this was *Operation Mallard.* IWM

SECURE AND DESTROY THE BRIDGES OVER THE DIVES AND THE DIVETTE

Suspended under his Albemarle

The mission to destroy these bridges was given to the sappers of the 3rd Parachute Squadron Royal Engineers, working alongside two paratroop battalions. Two gliders brought in jeeps and handcarts to facilitate the transportation of the demolition equipment and allow them to reach the objectives more quickly. In addition, the containers were fitted with a light signalling system to enable easier recovery at night, assuming that they did not fall and sink into water. With the bad

Aviation also provided considerable support: by bombing the communication centres, it aimed to delay the German reserves heading for the front line. NARA

marking of the *DZ*s, most of the Eureka beacons and lamps having been damaged during the drop, dropping Hill's 3rd Brigade battalions turned out to be more chaotic than the 5th Brigade's drop. One hundred and eight C-47s and seventeen gliders had to carry Hill's two thousand five hundred men to *DZ* K and V. The Advance Party, transported by sixteen Albemarles, was severely hampered by German anti-aircraft fire. One plane, having been hit, was forced to turn back to England. The shell that hit the aircraft had blown Major Collingwood out of the plane as he was preparing to jump. Suspended under the Albemarle with his parachute straps wrapped around his legs and a 30 kilo bag hanging below him, Collingwood had to wait half an hour before the other paratroops were able to hoist him back on board. Not at all put off by this ordeal, he took off again that day, arriving in Normandy in a glider.

However, the rest of the Advance Party managed to prepare for the airdrop of

Other paras also survived the D-Day airdrops after some frightening experiences, like Sapper Thomas who, wounded while he was still hanging from his parachute, managed to kill his three attackers by throwing a grenade at them.

the main part of the brigade. The gliders landing with the HQ and heavy weapons had some setbacks and did not all arrive at *DZ* V. The invasion identity stripes were not sufficient to prevent some terrible mistakes. One warship opened fire on a Dakota, upon which the crew, believing they were already over France, dropped their bombs: this was very unusual for this type of aircraft, and only strengthened the sailors' conviction that it was a Luftwaffe plane. The anti-aircraft fire doubled in intensity. Three paras jumped, only to disappear in the depths of the Channel.

Mission accomplished at Troarn and Bures

Pearson's 8th Battalion was dispersed within a wide perimeter around Touffréville. Thirteen of the twenty sticks jumped over *DZ* K instead of *DZ* N. At his rallying point to the west of Touffréville, Pearson found himself with only about thirty paras around him. Nevertheless, at the end of two and a half hours, he had managed to assemble one hundred and eighty men, with two PIATs, two

jeeps and four radios. Although himself injured in the hand and, at first without the Royal Engineers sappers who should have been helping him, Pearson headed for his objectives, the bridges at Bures and Troarn. On the way to Bures, the group met some sappers commanded by Captain Juckes, so they were then able to carry out their mission. The two bridges (a steel railway bridge and a road bridge) were blown up at 09:15. These sappers were themselves separated from another group of sixty men, of whom forty were Royal Engineers, led by Major Roseveare. Nine of these men, mounted in a jeep with a trailer, headed for Troarn. They reached there before Pearson's men, around 4 o'clock in the morning. Then followed one of the most spectacular episodes of D-Day. Far from arriving at Troarn discreetly, Roseveare's jeep crashed into a German roadblock, guarded by a sentry, at the outskirts of the town and it took more than twenty minutes for the paras to disentangle the barbed wire that had become wrapped around their jeep. The Germans were now alerted, all the more so after a cyclist was shot by a sten gun. Under the light of the German flares, the overloaded jeep was struggling up the main street, when a deluge of fire met the airborne group. The shots seemed to come from every door and window of the street, which seemed to go for ever. The driver put his foot down to escape from this hell while his passengers sprayed the walls with their own fire. The jeep hurtled down the slope leading to the bridge at more than 80 km/h. By some miracle, Roseveare and his men arrived at the bridge unharmed. One man was missing: Sapper Peachey, thrown out of the trailer which had swung wildly to and fro while the jeep was going flat out. Reaching the bridge, Roseveare quickly set the charges for the explosion, which caused a breach of 5 metres wide. The group did not get back to Bures until 5 o'clock, driving through the marshes, where the jeep had become bogged down.

Keep the enemy awake

Meanwhile Pearson, who had not received confirmation of Roseveare's success and knowing the orders, took it upon himself to carry out the mission. He therefore sent Captain Juckes' sappers to Troarn with a section of B Company, 8th Battalion. Street fighting broke out. Juckes found that although the explosive charges set by Roseveare had blown a hole in it, the road remained intact between the central pillar and the bank. At 15:00 hours, a new detonation considerably widened the breach, which then measured 23 metres. In the late afternoon, dug in in the Bures and Bavent woods, Pearson had scarcely half of his complement left - seventeen officers and three hundred men. The energetic commander of the 8th Battalion did not intend to let the enemy discover the weakness of his force, undertaking an active defence by sending out patrols to keep the enemy on full alert.

A success for the Canadian paras

Another unit of the 3rd Brigade, the 1st Canadian Battalion were no more successful in their drop over *DZ* V, where the 9th Battalion were also dropped. During the crossing, Sergeant Reid found that although there had been attempts to relax the atmosphere by resorting to their customary humour, the jokes fell flat. The men remained silent, immersed in their own thoughts. By contrast, the atmosphere was more light-hearted in Lance-Sergeant Feduk's plane, where jokes flew to and fro and they sang songs. Unfortunately for him, standing in the door with a 40 kilo bag containing a dismantled Bren gun, he was thrown out into the void when the plane suddenly

The plane carrying Sergeant Rice shook from the effect of flak exploding. The paras wanted to open the door and jump. He had to use all his powers of persuasion to calm them down; it was important to wait for the green light or risk parachuting into the Channel. In fact, Rice and his companions were dropped at Colleville-sur-Orne (later to become Colleville-Montgomery), much too far to the west and in the middle of the amphibious landing zone. They would have to endure the preparatory bombardment for the amphibious operation.

A parachutist of the Canadian battalion: the overall appearance was similar to that of the British airborne troops. Coll. Tanguy Le Sant

**Wherever possible, for example at Varaville,
the Germans relied on concreted positions. NARA**

swerved; consequently he became isolated. The Canadians' drop was indeed turbulent. The Eureka beacons were effectively unserviceable, so the navigation had to be carried out visually. But the green lights of the Pathfinders were barely visible, because of smoke from the explosions resulting from the bombardment of the nearby Merville battery. Only seventeen of the seventy-one aircraft carrying the 1st Canadian and 9th Battalion found *DZ V*. One stick even parachuted west of the Orne, in the sector assigned to the forces landing on *Sword Beach*. Nevertheless, though isolated, small groups of Canadian paras under the leadership of some motivated captains and lieutenants quickly re-grouped. Others suffered a more sinister fate: five Canadian paras were summarily shot by soldiers of the Wehrmacht.

A few Canadians, led by Major McLeod and then by Captain Hanson, still managed to seize Varaville, even though it took a ten hour fight to silence a casemate and the château defences. Forty-three Germans were taken prisoners. When they saw the numbers of their victors, they were unhappy to have been captured by an inferior force. In the small hours of the

Godfrey Maddison landed in a tangle of barbed wire. Entangled in the wires and handicapped by the weight of his equipment (he was carrying four mortar shells) he had to use all his resources of patience and skill to get out of his difficult position.

morning, the bridges at Robehomme and Varaville were able to be destroyed. At Robehomme, as soon as his mission was completed, Captain Jack displayed his stiff upper lip by settling down quietly to prepare breakfast with his men even though the area had not been secured. Leading by example; there was nothing like it for boosting the confidence of the paras and that of the French civilians toward their liberators. However, the charges had only shaken the bridge, which was not permanently destroyed until 06:00 hours, when Lieutenant Inman arrived with five sappers bringing 100 kilos of explosives (only 15 kilos had been used by Sergeant Poole for the first attempt). The 224th Parachute Field Ambulance had a more difficult time in the same sector. Some of them had been dropped a short distance from Varaville, their destination, but many landed in the marshes, their equipment was lost. Some, the less fortunate, drowned. The second section, under the orders of Captain Marquis, touched land 20 kilometres too far to the east. It took them several days, moving only at night in the marshes, helped by their toggle ropes (the individual rope carried by every para) and their life jackets, to join the men of the 1st Canadian Battalion.

Le Mesnil, a major objective on D-Day because of its heights which dominated Sword Beach, was the setting for a rare feat of arms, but which was to be repeated several times during the Battle of Normandy. Having mustered less than forty paras, lined up in a ditch facing three farm buildings held by the Germans at the crossroads, Captain Griffin gave the order: "Fix bayonets! Charge!"

The liberators arrived at last: Norman civilians and paras of the 12th Bn near Ranville on June 10. IWM

The audacious assault failed: two Germans did not hesitate to come out to finish off the wounded. However, although the Canadians suffered eight dead and thirteen wounded, fifty Germans had been killed, finally forcing the survivors to abandon the farm and concede the crossroads to their opponents.

After having kicked a football painted like Hitler's head into the Channel, Brigadier Hill, with units of his HQ, jumped at the same time as the Canadians. But, cut off, he floundered through the marshes for four hours before reaching the rendezvous point.

THE ASSAULT ON THE MERVILLE BATTERY

Reconnaisance before the assault

After an hour and ten minutes of flight, the Advance Party of Otway's 9th Battalion jumped over the objective. The mission of this small group of men, called the Troubridge Party after the name of an officer sent to reconnoitre the French fleet at Trafalgar in 1805, was to arrive first at the battery, observe the garrison's activities and movements, cut the barbed wire and clear a passage through the minefield. The Pathfinders were able to infiltrate silently, close to the German sentries and listen to them without making a noise. Without their equipment, they had been obliged to locate the mines with their

Some sources say that a first assault by paras - an isolated group? - was launched against the Merville battery at 01:00, which seems very early, resulting in about twenty German dead. This report is unclear.

hands and to mark the cleared corridors with their boots and knives. They then had to make their way back to report to Lieutenant-Colonel Otway.

Less than one third of the troops on the spot

The 9th Battalion, 3rd Brigade suffered the most widely scattered drop. Flak was responsible for disrupting the formation of the transport aircraft squadrons. They were going to have to jump in a sky criss-crossed with bullets and tracer shells. Some paras, who had been singing "There'll always be an England, and England shall be free" just a few moments earlier began to concentrate, anxious about the ordeal ahead. Sergeant Garrett's stick, aboard the C-47 'Molly Ho!' jumped

45 minutes late, after having demanded that the pilots make a second pass. In fact, they had needed to free a rifle, which had become wedged in the door frame after a round of flak hit them. In common with many paras that night, Terry Jeep nearly drowned in the marshes. He owed his survival to his reflex action of cutting the straps holding the two medical bags that he was carrying. Otway, who had generously passed round some Scotch to his companions on the plane, had a difficult parachute drop, as did most of his men. He landed in the garden of a house full of Germans: he could see them in the first floor rooms, preparing to come out. But one of the paras accompanying Otway had the quick reaction of throwing a brick through the window. The Germans, thinking it was a grenade, lay flat on the floor, giving the paras their opportunity to escape. Further away, in the flooded area, Otway attempted to rescue a para trapped in the mud, but the unfortunate man was sucked

Terence Otway stormed the Merville battery with his 9th Bn: a meticulously prepared mission.

under in a terrible scene recalling the testimonies of the '*poilus*' (French infantry) at Verdun. At the rendezvous point, Lieutenant-Colonel Otway was baffled: only 150 men out of the 550 in his battalion had assembled. By the end of August, 192 men

THE TERRIBLE EXPERIENCE OF PRIVATE TONY MEAD

He was actually impaled on a sharp branch in the top of a tree. Suffering terribly, Mead was able to unhook his equipment bags and cut the hangers of his parachute, which was wrapped around a nearby tree. Despite his pain, he managed to extricate himself, and climbed methodically down the trunk to the last branch before dropping the last five or six metres! Refusing to be left out when a signals sergeant offered to take him to find medical care, he stood up and, Sten in hand, set off.

This paratroop seems to have crash-landed: in fact he had just fallen over after coming into contact with the ground. This photograph, taken in Holland, reminds us how dangerous an operational jump was. US Army

were still missing: prisoners of the Germans or drowned in the marshes. Worse still, the five gliders carrying their equipment (mine detectors, jeeps, mortars, machine guns, etc.) had crashed into the sea. Lance-Corporal Green and Privates Jepp and Penstone landed in error at Franceville-Plage. Hidden by the French, they reached the mouth of the River Orne by swimming. After being rearmed and re-equipped, it was June 24 before they rejoined their unit.

Attack!

Otway could wait no longer without failing in his mission. He took stock of his heavy weapons: single Vickers; he also had a few Bangalore torpedoes (20 instead of 180). However, he had no other choice than to carry out the attack with what he had. What was more, he could not count on the gliders: Gordon-Brown's Horsa was far away, a second missed its target and the third, commanded by Hugh Pond, was hit by flak when it flew over the battery. Avoiding a mine field at the very last minute, the glider broke in two and, with its tail section in flames, crashed in an orchard.

04:30 Dawn was approaching: they had to attack quickly. The Vickers machine gun in Sergeant McGeever's hands would support the left flank. On the right, a Bren provided covering fire and a group led by Sergeant Knight, armed with another Bren, created a diversion at the main entrance of the battery. The Bangalore torpedoes exploded, twisting and tearing the barbed wire. Attack! At the signal, the paras, led by Major Parry, rushed forwards and charged to take the enemy positions. Six German machine guns replied with devastating fire (a Tobruk machine gun on casemate no.1 was particularly lethal) but McGeever's Vickers silenced three of them. Revolver in hand, Lieutenant Jefferson sounded the charge with his hunting horn. They had first to cross a minefield where they did not see the safe paths, since there were no marker ribbons on the ground. They had to force their way through the network of barbed wire up to the blockhouse: above all else they had to avoid becoming entangled in it. Two groups selected for each of the two breaches had to lie flat to make way for the following waves. Shots were flying everywhere. The German machine gun crews tried to take the attackers in enfilade, and from their various positions laid down cross-fire. The sounds of explosions mingled with the screams of the wounded. Craters dotted the ground: they were a blessing for taking shelter. Otway was in the thick of it, with bullets whistling all round him: one ricocheted off his water bottle while another brushed past his uniform. Then it was hand-to-hand combat. Arriving at the casemates, the paras threw grenades into the ventilation ducts and then into the bunkers. Bursts of firing from submachine guns flew everywhere: there was nothing but smoke, dust, screaming and swearing. In groups of six, instead of the thirty envisaged by the plan, the paras neutralised the casemates one by one. The courage and training of the British paras

prevailed over the stubborn, brave defence by the German gunners. Shells fell within the battery's perimeter. The German machine gun crews fought on to the end, before being neutralised. The paras then had to disable the battery's artillery pieces, using plastic explosives on the breeches. The guns were only 100mm, not 150mm as had been expected. Major Parry received his officer's reports: all the guns had been destroyed; the mission was accomplished. Otway gave the order to withdraw. Seventy men were killed or wounded, half of the paras involved in the action. Only twenty-two Germans were taken prisoner, out of a garrison of approximately one hundred and thirty gunners and engineers, perhaps even two hundred. The Royal Navy liaison officer had become lost in the drop. Unable to contact the fleet, he knew that HMS Arethusa would open fire at 05:50. However, they were able to send up a yellow Very signal, and to release a carrier pigeon which would reach London safely.

The day still had plenty of events in store for Otway's battalion of seventy to eighty men. The withdrawal began at 06:00: it turned out to be difficult and some skirmishes took place. The 9th Battalion had orders to destroy a radar installation at Sallenelles, but, given his depleted force, Otway decided first to march on Le Plein. Heavy fighting took place in Le Plein, and Otway dug in around the Chateau d'Amfreville. The success of the assault on the Merville battery has to be tempered by the fact that the site was re-occupied by the Germans, who were able to repair two of the 100mm guns.

CONSOLIDATE THE BRIDGEHEAD

Ranville secured

Arriving at *DZ* N at 00:50, Johnson's 12th and Luard's 13th Battalions, were heading respectively towards Ranville and Bas-de-Ranville. At 02:30, half of the 12th Battalion was assembled at its rallying point, the Écarde quarry, one kilometre to the north-west of Ranville bridge. The intelligence officer of the 12th Battalion used his signalling lamp to indicate the rendezvous zone for the dispersed paras. The firing of a German armoured vehicle soon forced him to stop this perilous practice. The paras then headed for their objective. By 04:00, Bas-de-Ranville was under the control of

Commandos reinforced the airborne bridgehead from June 6: defensive positions had to be prepared at once. IWM

**Soldiers of N° 3 Commando dug in near
the wreckage of gliders at la Haute Ecarde.** IWM

Lieutenant-Colonel Johnson's men. The fighting there became very fierce when the Germans counter-attacked. The paras held their positions but it would not have taken much for them to have been overcome. Positioned in a forward post on a hedge with twelve men, Captain Sim pushed back a strong enemy attack which was supported by two self-propelled guns. Fortunately, in addition to two PIATs, the paras had a

For Raymond Batten, a private in this battalion, his arrival in Normandy was disconcerting. Parachuted into a wood, he remained suspended in a tree, without weapons (he had lost his Sten in the drop), at the mercy of German patrols. A silhouette suddenly appeared, approached and then went on its way. Batten, who had pretended to be dead, was then able to climb down from his tree. He headed for his battalion's rallying point, listening for the sound of a hunting horn, discovered the body of a para whose parachute had not opened, and came across another para screaming with rage at having lost a friend, killed by the enemy.

six-pound anti-tank gun: a soldier crawled up to Sim to warn him that, unfortunately, the breech was not working and they were unable to fire. Their losses were increasing and Sim had to fall back to a ditch before returning with reinforcements to re-take the hedge. In the meantime, another six-pound anti-tank gun had reduced the two self-propelled guns to smouldering wrecks. The situation was much the same on the whole of the front held by the 12th Battalion. The Germans, determined, even infiltrated Bas-de-Ranville before being pushed back. The British ranks were strengthened early in the afternoon when reinforcements arrived.

"Tally Ho!"

Isolated men from the 12th Bn return after spending three days behind the German lines: well worth a cup of tea! IWM

Rallying to the sound of a hunting horn and shouting their battle cry: "Tally-ho!", the 13th Battalion took Ranville at 02:30, according to plan. Another hunting call announced the taking of the village. The other task for the battalion was to prepare and secure the landing ground for the Divisional HQ and the indispensable anti-tank guns; it was carried out by A Company under Major Cramphorn, assisted by the sappers. In this sector, the German response was erratic, starting at 01:30 with mortars and machine-gun fire coming from Sallenelles. The drop had been fairly successful since half the men had jumped over the *DZ*. As with their comrades of the 12th, the paras of the 13th had a much more difficult time when it came to repelling the counter-attacks of the 21 Panzer. The six-pound anti-tank guns proved essential here in breaking the enemy's momentum, more particularly during an assault supported by four Sturmgeschützen (in fact built on Lorraine chassis).

THE ARRIVAL OF AIRBORNE REINFORCEMENTS BY GLIDER

HQ and the guns arrive

American glider landings, like this one, were not without their problems. It seemed that the arrival of the British gliders was carried out more easily, overall. The fields were wider, and not under German control. NARA

At 03:35, after nearly two hours of work, the sappers of 591 (Antrim) Parachute Squadron Royal Engineers and paras of the 13th Battalion cleared the last of 'Rommel's asparagus' as fifty gliders, out of the sixty-eight Horsas and four Hamilcars which had left England, landed on *LZ* N, near Ranville. The Pathfinders of the 22nd Independent Parachute Company had set out flares every 90 metres along the 1,000 metres of each of the two landing strips. One thousand two hundred men were aboard the approaching gliders, bringing with them the artillery pieces. Major-General Gale, who had taken a one-hour nap during the crossing, was sitting in Horsa no.70, piloted by Major Griffiths. Their arrival was impressive: the Horsa dived almost vertically then flew in a circle while heading to the ground where it touched down, bounced and finally stopped against an embankment. The arrival of the gliders was somewhat confused: some Horsas collided while others managed to avoid each other and, from everywhere, came the distressed cries of the wounded and the sound of

Just after releasing from its towing plane, Staff Sergeant Pearce's Horsa collided with another glider, a few dozen metres off the ground. He managed to keep control of his glider, however, and landed in a cultivated field. "Time we had a cup of tea!" said his co-pilot.

breaking timber. One glider crashed, burying itself in a house, wakening a little girl, Giselle Tanguy, who saw with horror the Horsa's cockpit and the body of its pilot. The last gliders landed, attracting more attention from enemy flak gunners, who had by then had the time to adjust their aim. What is more, the landing strips were becoming congested. Staff-Sergeant Proctor was coming in to land his glider in an area bristling with 'Rommel's asparagus': when he noticed that they were methodically and regularly planted, he was able to land in the gaps between them.

Two hours later, by 05:20, nearly 5,600 soldiers of the 6th Airborne were in Normandy (60 Pathfinders, 180 men with John Howard, 200 men of the Advance Party, 4,000 paratroops and 1,200 men flown in by gliders). In addition, 17 guns, 44 jeeps, 55 motorcycles and a bulldozer had arrived. The airdrop of a Tetrarch light tank was a failure. The 6th Airborne's HQ was installed at about 06:00 at the Château de Hom, at Bas-de-Ranville, becoming fully operational once they heard the bombardment preliminary to the landing at *Sword Beach*: radio silence could be broken. Gale had every reason to be satisfied as everything seemed to be going according to plan.

Mass arrival of gliders in the evening of D-Day

Two other landing strips at *DZ* N had to be operational before the end of the day so the sappers and paratroops continued their efforts, clearing the field of the debris of gliders and filling in holes, with the help of their sole Clark bulldozer, which had arrived undamaged in the night. This type of bulldozer had been used with success by Wingate in Burma. Towards 21:00 hours, *Operation Mallard* brought in reinforcements: the 6th Airlanding Brigade (more than 2,000 men), guns, tanks, vehicles and equipment on board 218 Horsas and 30 Hamilcars. They landed at *LZ* N (142 gliders) near Ranville, and at *LZ* W (106 gliders) near Saint-Aubin-d'Arquenay, to the west of the Orne. A few Horsa gliders did not reach *LZ* W: two landed in England, a third became lost and another landed in the English Channel. Five soldiers managed to scramble into an inflatable raft but the currents drove them ashore at Merville, where they were taken prisoner by the Germans. The flights and landings in daylight had few difficulties, apart from some flak and a few accidents. Many photographs bear witness to this arrival, 'like an exercise', of a number of gliders, completely intact. At Ranville, on *LZ* N, the 142 Horsas and

Fields covered with gliders: the airborne section of *Operation Overlord* was a success. IWM

Hamilcars all landed within half an hour. The Hamilcars, thirty of them, carried Tetrach light tanks in their holds. Eleven of these tanks became caught up in the many parachutes still scattered over the area and their tracks came off! To make matters worse, two tanks were lost when a landing Hamilcar finished up by careering into another which had just landed. On the evening of 6th, 7,900 men of the 6th Airborne had arrived in Normandy. Three hundred fifty-four gliders were used. All that was missing were some units which arrived by sea on June 7.

By the evening of the 'Longest Day', the division was solidly established at the bridgehead. To the west, the 5th Parachute Brigade was established, as planned, on the line extending from Bas-de-Ranville to Ranville. To the east, the 3rd Parachute Brigade were defending a 6 kilometre front from Le Plein to the Bois de Bavent, passing through Le Mesnil. The 1st Special Service Brigade, as well as reinforcing the paratroops and the airborne troops of the 6th Airlanding Brigade, was to be deployed the next day to the south-west of the narrow bridgehead on the Orne.

CASUALTIES

OVERALL: A POSITIVE CASUALTY LIST

The first reports relating to airborne operations were reasonably reassuring for the SHAEF commanders. Leigh-Mallory, who had predicted a disaster resulting in heavy losses, had the courtesy to write a letter of apology to Eisenhower: "Words fail me to express my joy in seeing that my fears have proved unfounded. Let me congratulate you on your enlightened choice." Of the 1,250 transport aircraft involved in the *Operation Neptune,* only 29 were lost.

The airdrop operation, involving more than 18,000 men, in the night of June 5 – 6, was a massive undertaking (in Sicily there had been only 3,400 paras of one unit, the 504th PIR). For the first time, the British committed an entire airborne division during a single parachute drop. The American airborne forces taking part in *Operation Neptune* totalled 13,300 paratroopers,

5,000 soldiers carried by gliders (counting the pilots, nearly half of whom arrived on June 7) and 5,700 members of the USAAF. By evening on D-Day, the 4th US ID, which had helped to secure the Exits from the most important beach, had landed successfully with only light losses. The objectives of the 82nd and 101st were broadly met, with the exception of a few bridges, which were blockaded by airborne troops although the plan had anticipated that these bridges would be secured on both banks. A considerable part of the 82nd Airborne remained isolated to the west of the Merderet. Within this Division, only the 505th PIR had fully completed its mission. By the evening of June 6, many units remained isolated and had not linked up everywhere with the forces landing from the sea. The Americans had nevertheless managed to establish a bridgehead in the

The black and white invasion stripes: one of the most ingenious identification systems. NARA

The USAAF insignia.
Coll. Tanguy Le Sant

The 8th Air Force insignia.
Coll. Tanguy Le Sant

The 9th Air Force insignia.
Coll. Tanguy Le Sant

C-47s of Captain William R. Cooper's 96th Troop Carrier Squadron fly above the invasion fleet at Utah Beach.
NARA

Airborne. Less widely dispersed than their American counterparts, the 7,900 British airborne had held the captured ground in the face of weak German counter-attacks. Reinforced by troops landed on *Sword Beach*, the 6th Airborne, of which not one battalion had remained isolated, was firmly established on the right bank of the Orne, ensuring the security of the eastern flank of the invasion. The support of the aerial forces harassing the enemy, and naval forces - a US Navy operator dropped with the American paras, enabling them to take advantage of the devastating fire from the cruiser USS Quincy - had largely contributed to the success of the airborne operation. The intervention of troops landed on the beaches was also crucial to the ultimate success of the airborne operations. In this way, while drawing the German's attention to themselves (the 21. Panzer was diverted from an attack on the 6th Airborne to counter the forces landed on *Sword Beach*) units which had participated in the amphibious assault rapidly reinforced the airborne troops. This was particularly the case for Task Force Raff on *Utah Beach* and the commandos of Lord Lovat's 1st Special Service Brigade on *Sword Beach*.

Cotentin. Meanwhile, the southern flank, towards Carentan, was not fully secured (Saint-Côme-du-Mont was strongly held by German paras). Kampfgruppe Meyer (the 352. ID's reserve), armed with tank destroyers and first directed to engage the American paras, received a counter-order to go into action at *Gold Beach*.

In spite of the heavy losses incurred on D-Day, the 6th Airborne had also accomplished all of its missions, and in a more noticeable way than the 82nd and 101st

THE 6ᵀᴴ AIRBORNE

The exact losses suffered by the 6th, 82nd and 101st Airborne on D-Day were very difficult to assess, due to the wide dispersal of the airdrops, the confused fighting and the large number of missing persons. It is estimated that the British lost 1,022 men,

of which 61 were killed, 349 wounded and 612 missing, out of a little over 7,000 men involved in the operation. By the 26th of August, its losses in Normandy had risen to 4,457 men: 821 killed, 2,709 wounded and 927 missing (including 878 prisoners).

As regards the 82nd and 101st Airborne, a study ordered by the US Army in August 1944, estimated that the losses on D-Day for the two airborne divisions were 2,499 men (182 killed, 557 wounded and 501 missing for the 101st; 156 killed, 347 wounded and 756 missing for the 82nd). This was out of a total of 15,600 airborne Americans deployed on D-Day, not counting the soldiers landed from the sea nor the 2,600 men flown in by gliders on D + 1. However, as at June 30, the losses amounted to 4,670 men for the 101st and to 4,480 for the 82nd, of which were 4,490 missing for both Divisions, most of these having been lost on June 6, killed or taken prisoner.

THE PATHFINDERS

The overall success of the airborne *Operation Neptune* should not overlook the severe setbacks which confronted the airborne troops. The first to stand on Normandy soil were the Pathfinders, who were thus the first to suffer serious difficulties. Some teams had not been dropped accurately: for the British, the Pathfinders for the three *DZ* had not landed in the right place. Even worse, those destined for *DZ* K landed at *DZ* N where they placed their Eureka beacons. As to the Pathfinders headed for *DZ* V (for the 3rd Parachute Brigade), one of the beacons had been damaged on landing and the second was dropped too far away to be of any use. However the British had used only a minimal number of Pathfinders - 60 - unlike the Americans, who had designated three teams for each regiment (one per battalion). The impossibility of using the equipment, or a marking error, had led to the bad navigational marking of the *DZ*s. Paradoxically, although the mission entrusted to the British Pathfinders was less successful overall, the 6th Airborne airdrops were relatively less scattered.

Losses of the three airborne divisions amounted to 3,500 men. NARA

THE NIGHT OF THE PARATROOPS (JUNE 6 1944)

AMERICAN AIRBORNE OPERATIONS (JUNE 6 1944)

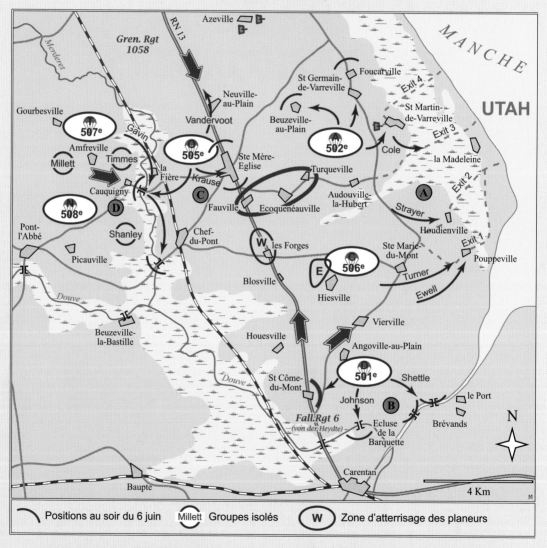

Positions au soir du 6 juin   Millett Groupes isolés   W Zone d'atterrissage des planeurs

The 82nd and the 101st Airborne were parachuted into the west flank of the invasion, in support of the landing on Utah Beach. By the evening of D-Day, the important crossroads of Sainte-Mère-Eglise had been taken, but several units were still isolated to the west of the Merderet. The wide dispersal of the parachute drops had been partly compensated for by the over-cautious German response. As can be seen on the map, the area was flooded and included several streams, over which crossing points had to be established.

BRITISH AIRBORNE OPERATIONS
(JUNE 6 1944)

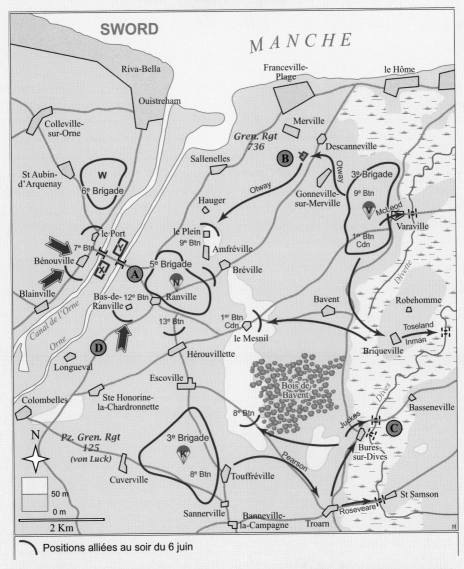

Positions alliées au soir du 6 juin

The 6th British Airborne was dropped to the east of the Orne, ensuring the safety of Sword Beach and the whole of the bridgehead. The map clearly shows the importance of the Orne and its canal, as well as the extent of the Dives marshes. By the evening of June 6, all objectives had been attained: the bridges had been destroyed or taken, the Merville battery had been neutralised and the division was firmly established in position.

DISPERSED PARACHUTE DROPS

Operation Neptune was blighted by very inaccurate airdrops. The loss of a large number of élite troops, who had so meticulously prepared for their mission, before they could engage the enemy was not a satisfactory outcome. The weather conditions were not ideal, as had been needed, and the paras were subject to the problems caused by strong winds. The Germans had lowered their guard precisely because of this bad weather, yet they had still been able to cause heavy losses to some units in the air. What would have happened if

Children making friends with their liberators: troops of the 101st US Airborne's 326th Airborne Engineer Battalion NARA

the German army had been expectantly awaiting the enemy attack, knowing that the invasion was in progress (in the event, it was the arrival of the airborne which sounded the alarm for the VII. Army)?

The inexperience of the pilots, the flak, the wind, the night, the DZs not being satisfactorily marked, the excessive speed of some aircraft at the time the paras jumped: so many reasons go towards explaining the widespread dispersal affecting the airdrops. In addition, many aircraft were flying without navigators, forcing the pilots to navigate for themselves. Radio silence prevented them from warning the following squadrons that the weather conditions were not of the best. Equipment and the supplies, dropped inside containers, wicker boxes or bags, were also widely dispersed and were, in addition, sometimes damaged or lost (for example by sinking in the marshes) when they landed. Some of the C-47s had been de-stabilised by over-loading, in particular the Parapacks under the wings.

Many sticks of the 82nd fell in the sector meant for the 101st and vice versa. Only ten per cent reached their DZ; almost half of the airborne troops were parachuted-in more than 4 miles away; some were even dropped dozens of kilometres from their objective. Only the 505th PIR could pride itself on a successful airdrop. The 501st PIR landed in a fairly concentrated pattern but suffered losses. In addition, a quantity of men and materials (including precious radios) disappeared in the Merderet marshes. The errors and confusion during the airdrops had a greater effect on the two American airborne divisions. The efforts needed to create order were much greater in comparison. At dawn, only 1,500 paras of the 82nd Airborne and 1,100 of the 101st Airborne had actually reached their objectives. Even the 6th Airborne, certainly less widely dispersed in the airdrop, encountered problems resulting from misplaced parachute drops.

THE CONSEQUENCES OF DISPERSION

The maze of hedges, the marshes and the lack of radios made assembling particularly difficult. However, some elements of the airborne divisions formed ad hoc groups determined to carry out their mission, regardless of their lack of numbers. They tried to reach the rallying points, or marched directly on the objective. Regrouping bit by bit, the paras managed to carry out their tasks. Everywhere, in the midst of chaos, could be seen the same scenes of leaders of all ranks, working hard to bring together all the troops they could muster, attacking the first opponents that the chance of battle sent their way.

To carry out their missions at the head of their battalion, many officers had to rely on a much reduced number of troops (instead of the 600 to 800 men according to the rolls) and little equipment. Colonel Johnson was able to assemble only 250 men of his 501st PIR (out of nearly 1,500 men in his two battalions). At Saint-Martin-de-Varreville, Lieutenant-Colonel Cole led the operations with 120 men of his 3/502nd (this rose to 250 by the evening of June 6), barely 80 being available to secure one of the Utah Beach exits. Lieutenant-Colonel Cassidy (1/502nd) and Lieutenant-Colonel Strayer (2/506th) were able to assemble only 200 men between them before separating. The same happened with the British: Pearson's 8th Battalion counted only 300 men by mid-afternoon on June 6 - barely half of the battalion. Lieutenant-Colonel Otway led the assault on the Merville battery with 150 men out of the 550 of his 9th Battalion. The senior officers of the airborne divisions had to improvise with considerably fewer troops than expected, but in the majority of cases, the missions were successful. The number of missing (killed or taken prisoner), directly due to the wide dispersion of the airdrops, remained very high at the end of the campaign, since it amounted to several thousands of men.

The lesson learned from these too widely scattered airdrops was, however, applied: there would never again be a night-time airdrop during a major airborne operation, not in Provence

American C-47s in the Dutch sky: the American paras had become experienced, since D-Day in Normandy. IWM

Market Garden exceeded *Operation Neptune* for the number of airborne troops, but the airdrops were spread out over several days. US Army

(*Dragoon*, August 15, 1944); not in Holland (*Market Garden*, September 17, 1944, which in any case was during the new moon) nor in Germany (*Varsity*, March 22, 1944). Those airdrops were considerably more successful and accurate than those of D-Day. Yet one of the few benefits of a night airdrop (although the night can be lit up by tracer bullets, explosions, searchlights and flares) is that it effectively provides the enemy with more difficult targets. What is more, the paras who came under enemy fire during their short but perilous descents decided that in future they would jump with loaded weapons in their hands.

THE IMPOSSIBLE GERMAN COUNTER-ATTACK

The presence of small, aggressive groups could seriously disrupt the movements of those enemy units patrolling areas which they could reasonably judge as being safe. Furthermore, the sightings of paratroops in several sectors prevented the German command from determining where the main airborne force was located. However, it was essential that they quickly mount a counter-attack. There was no front or flanks, a very disconcerting state of affairs for many German officers.

Luck was on the side of the Allied paras. Friedrich Dollmann, commander of the VII. Army, had organised a Kriegspiel (a

The Fallschirmjäger, the German paras, had to fight their American counterparts after June 6. Coll. Tanguy Le Sant

map exercise) in Rennes, on June 6. All the senior officers from Normandy and Brittany were to attend. Half of the divisional commanding officers and a quarter of the regimental commanders were on their way there when *Operation Overlord* began. General Hellmich of the 243 ID, General Schlieben of the 709 ID, and General Falley of the 91 Luftlande-Division, which is to say the commanders of all three divisions defending the Cotentin, had to attend. General der Artillerie Marcks, commander of the LXXXIV Korps, which was defending the west of Basse-Normandie, was also obliged to go. But reports of air incursions and enemy airdrops were multiplying in the night of this June 6. At 02:15, General Max Pemsel, the 7th. Army Chief of Staff, placed the units on a state of alert.

Yet the German divisions defending the Cotentin Peninsula were not able to mount large scale, coordinated counter-attacks on this fateful day. Scattered, the Fallschirmjäger of Major von der Heydte were also slow going into action. The death of General Falley only added to the confusion in the German camp. The available reserves in the vicinity, in Calvados, were not able to intervene. Alerted at 03:15, General Kraiss, who commanded the 352 ID, sent the Kampfgruppe Meyer to Carentan, on Marcks' orders, to intercept the American airborne. If the landing took place, he thought, this would be at high tide; the Kampfgruppe therefore had time to neutralise the enemy paratroops and then take up position to oppose the landing. An error of judgment: the amphibious assault took place at mid-tide, much earlier than expected. When the assault on the beaches started, Meyer was recalled towards first *Omaha*, and then *Gold Beach* before he was able to engage the American airborne forces.

July 9, 1944: a Sherman passes the wreckage of two of Das Reich's Panzer IVs. What would have happened to the airborne Allies if the German army had been able to strike hard with its Panzers on June 6? NARA

around 02:30, but a PIAT destroyed the leading tank destroyer. A timid intervention by the heavy Panzergrenadiere-Regiment 192 of the 21st Panzerdivision was no more successful. The fighting was much more violent to the east of the Orne. The Germans attacked in strength south of Ranville throughout the morning. The paras of the 6th Airborne however had the good fortune to confront only a part of the 21st Panzer. It was 08:00 hours before the German division's tank regiment set off with the mission of destroying the British airborne bridgehead east of the Orne. But a counter-order was received at 09:30, about turn, back across the Orne and head west, for a counter-attack at the beaches. It is clear that a more vigorous action on the part of the 21st Panzerdivision would have sounded the death knell of the *Red Devils* and weakened the Allied bridgehead because of the threat which would then have menaced its right flank. As for the Panzers' strategic reserves, they did not intervene on June 6. The decisive battle that Rommel wanted for D-Day, at the very moment where the enemy set foot on the continent, would not take place ...

The British paras also benefited from this confusion, which had paralysed the enemy. The 21st Panzerdivision remained totally passive as the hours ticked by. Major Luck asked permission to carry out a counter-attack but had to wait for the return of the Divisional Commander, General Feuchtinger, who was visiting his mistress in Paris. At Bénouville, the Germans tried to regain control of the bridge. The anti-tank company of the 716 ID attacked

THE GLIDERS

One fact is clear in the case of the 6th Airborne: unlike the parachute drops, the landing of airborne troops and equipment by gliders was carried out without great dispersion. Most of the gliders arrived at their intended locations. But few of those carrying heavy weapons and materials reached their objectives and a number of them crashed on landing. Recognising the fragility of the Horsa and its unfortunate tendency to break up on landing (340 GIs were lost on board these aircraft, as against only 123 on board Wacos), the Americans decided not to use the British glider in future. None of the Horsas used by the Americans on D-Day were able to be put back into service, as were most of the Wacos. The operation to tow them back to England did not begin until June 23; by then 97% of the gliders were unrecoverable.

The American Staff planners were nevertheless reasonably satisfied with the way the missions had gone. It had been proved that the gliders were able to carry artillery pieces (95 in all over June 6 and 7) and materiel, and this in spite of the bad weather, and the bad visibility due to the landings not being carried out in daylight.

However, the missions on June 7 showed that daylight landings were more precise and less prone to accidents, while the danger represented by the enemy during daytime landings seemed to have been over-estimated during the preparations for *Operation Neptune.*

THE BRIDGES AND ENEMY BATTERIES

The Canadian and British paratroops managed to seize the bridges on the River Orne and its canal as well as destroying all the bridges they had as their objectives on the Dives and the Divette. The Americans experienced the greatest difficulties. Although the exits from *Utah Beach*, several bridges, and the lock at La Barquette were well controlled on both banks, some bad decisions taken by certain commanders prevented the paratroops taking control of

the Merderet at the bridges at La Fière and Chef-du-Pont. Several batteries (Saint-Martin-de-Varreville, Le Holdy, Brécourt, Merville, etc) had been silenced. Meticulously prepared, the storming of the Merville battery by the 9th Battalion was certainly a success, but Otway, bitter, never accepted the heavy losses suffered during the assault or during the airdrops. He held the RAF responsible, and the taking of the battery did nothing to change his point of view.

A bridge over the Soule, south of Coutances. The airborne troops showed themselves capable of capturing engineering works, thanks to coups de main. NARA

Operation Deadstick , led by John Howard, was the airborne troops' greatest success on June 6, 1944. This alone justified the commitment of the airborne troops on 'The Longest Day'. IWM

THE *COUP DE MAIN* LED BY JOHN HOWARD

We finish this book with the operation with which we started: the taking of the Bénouville and Ranville bridges. The success of this mission alone symbolises the professionalism of the Allied airborne troops who unquestionably deserve to be called an élite force. Certainly luck and the element of surprise went in Howard's favour. Meticulous preparation and highly accurate intelligence, with regard to the information provided by the Resistance and aerial photographs, also explain the final success to a large extent. The arrival of the 7th Battalion in reinforcement was also decisive. *Operation Deadstick,* conducted more in the tradition of German airborne troops than British (a direct assault on an objective of high military value), was an undeniable success. The risk of incurring higher losses was certainly increased but the capture of the objective was assured. This lesson was not learned, and represented the major difference between *Neptune* and *Market Garden,* where the airborne force was dropped too far from its major objectives, in particular the bridges at Arnhem and Nijmegen. The *Comet* plan, abandoned on September 10 in favour of *Market Garden,* had allowed for three '*Coup de Main*' parties of three gliders each at the bridges of Arnhem, Nijmegen and Graves.

APPENDICES

Appendix I
SCHEDULE OF PARACHUTE DROPS AND LANDINGS

6th British Airborne

00:15 - Major Howard's 180 men in
6 Horsa gliders

00:20 - 60 Pathfinders on board 6 Albemarles
200 men of the Advance Parties of the 3rd
and 5th Parachute Brigades (16 Albemarles)

00:50 - 2,500 Paras of the 3rd Brigade with
108 C-47s and 17 gliders
2,600 Paras of the 5th Brigade with 91 Stirlings
HQ Division with 21 C-47s and 19 Albemarles

03:20 - 1,200 men of the HQ (artillery, engineering, medical)
in 68 Horsa gliders and 4 Hamilcars

04:30 - Three Horsa gliders on the Merville battery

21:00 - Mallard; 2,000 men in
248 Horsa and Hamilcar gliders

101st US Airborne

00:16 - Pathfinders

00:48 - *Albany*: 6,928 men (6,750 dropped)
in 433 C-47s

04:00 - *Chicago*: 259 troops and pilots in 52 Wacos

21:00 - *Keokuk*: 221 troops and pilots in 32 Horsas

82nd Airborne

00:20 - Pathfinders

01:20 - Boston: 6,928 men (6,750 dropped)
from 378 C-47s

04:07 - Detroit: 326 troops and pilots
in 53 Wacos

21:00 - *Elmira*: 1,542 troops and pilots
in 140 Horsas and 36 Wacos

Appendix II
NUMBERS OF GLIDERS USED ON JUNE 6

6th Airborne: 354 gliders

Howard's '*Coup de Main*': 6 gliders.
Arrived with the 3rd Parachute Brigade:
17 gliders.
Arrived with the HQ during *Operation Tonga*:
72 gliders.
Assault on the Merville battery: 3 gliders.
6th Airlanding Brigade (*Operation Mallard*):
256 gliders.

82nd and 101st Airborne: 313 gliders*

Detroit: 53 gliders.
Chicago: 52 gliders.
Keokuk: 32 gliders.
Elmira: 176 gliders.

* Other gliders used within Overlord: 203 American
gliders landed on June 7 during missions Galveston and
Hackensack

Appendix III
ORDER OF BATTLE OF
THE 6th BRITISH AIRBORNE *RED DEVILS*

Commanding Officer: Major-General Gale
Assistant commanding: Captain Haughton
Chief of Staff: Lieutenant-Colonel Hickie
GSO1 (OPS): Lieutenant-Colonel Bray
GSO1 (Air): Lieutenant-Colonel Bradish
GSO2 (OPS): Major Baird
GSO2 (Intelligence): Major Lacoste
GSO3 (OPS): Captain Spurling
GSO3 (Air): Captain Pratt
GSO3 (Intelligence): Captain Max
Intelligence Corps: Captain Scholes; Captain Clarke
317th Field Security Section: Captain Donaldson-London; Captain McMillan.
Glider Pilot Regiment: Brigadier Chatterton
22nd Independent Para Company:
  Major Lennox-Boyd (killed on June 6).

3rd Para Brigade: Brigadier Hill
Second: Major Collingwood
8th Battalion Parachute Regiment: Colonel Pearson
9th Battalion Parachute Regiment: Lieutenant-Colonel
  Otway; Lieutenant-Colonel Crokenden.
1st Canadian Parachute Battalion: Lieutenant-Colonel
  Bradbrooke; Lieutenant-Colonel Nicholson

5th Para Brigade: Brigadier Poett
  Second: Major Lough
7th Battalion Parachute Regiment:
  Lieutenant-Colonel Pine-Coffin
12th Yorkshire Battalion Parachute Regiment:
  Lieutenant-Colonel Johnson
13th Battalion Parachute Regiment:
  Lieutenant-Colonel Luard

6th Airlanding Brigade:
  Brigadier the Honourable Kindersley
Second: Colonel Parker
12th Battalion Devonshire Regiment:

Lieutenant-Colonel Stevens
2nd Battalion Oxfordshire and Buckinghamshire Light
  Infantry: Lieutenant-Colonel Roberts
1st Battalion Royal Ulster Rifles:
  Lieutenant-Colonel Carson

Support units and services:
  6th A/B Armoured Recce Regiment:
  Lieutenant-Colonel Stuart
6th A/B Division Signals:
  Lieutenant-Colonel Smallman-Tew
Royal Army Ordnance Corps:
  Lieutenant-Colonel Watson

Royal Army Medical Corps:
  Colonel MacEwan
Royal Artillery: Lieutenant-Colonel Norris
2nd Airlanding Anti-Aircraft Battery: Major Rowat
3rd Airlanding Anti-Tank Battery: Major Cranmer
4th Airlanding Anti-Tank Battery: Major Dixon
2nd Forward Observation Unit: Major Rice
53rd Airlanding Regiment RA:
  Lieutenant-Colonel Teacher
210th Airlanding Light Battery RA:
  Major the Honourable Russell
211th Airlanding Light Battery RA: Major Craigie
212th Airlanding Light Battery RA: Major Gubbins

Royal Engineers (RE): Lieutenant-Colonel Lowman

Royal Electrical and Mechanical Engineers (REME):
  Lieutenant-Colonel Powditch
6th A/B Division Workshop REME: Major Bonniwell
286th Workshop Company Royal Army Service Corps:
  Lieutenant-Colonel Lovegrove
63rd Airborne Composite Company: Major Billetop
398th Airborne Composite Company: Major Phipps
716th Airborne Composite Company: Major Jones

Appendix IV
ORDER OF BATTLE
OF THE 82ND US AIRBORNE *ALL AMERICANS*

Commanding Officer: Major General Ridgway.
Assistant Division Commander: Brigadier-General Gavin.
Assistant Division Commander: Brigadier-General Howell.

Chief of Staff: Colonel Eaton (wounded on June 6 and
  replaced by Colonel Raff).
G 1. Lieutenant-Colonel Schellhammer.

G 2. Lieutenant-Colonel Whitfield.
G 3. Lieutenant-Colonel Wienecke.
G 4. Lieutenant-Colonel Zinn.
Pathfinders : Major Roberts.

505th PIR : Colonel Ekman.
1/505th : Major Kellam (killed on June 6).
2/505th : Lieutenant-Colonel Vandervoort (wounded on June 6).
3/505th : Lieutenant-Colonel Krause.

507th PIR : Colonel Millet (fait prisonnier le 8 juin et remplacé par le Lieutenant-Colonel Maloney).
1/507th : Lieutenant-Colonel Ostberg (wounded on June 6).
2/507th : Lieutenant-Colonel Timmes.
3/507th : Lieutenant-Colonel Maloney.

508th PIR : Colonel Lindquist.
1/508th : Lieutenant-Colonel Batcheller (killed on June 6).
2/508th : Lieutenant-Colonel Shanley.
3/508th : Lieutenant-Colonel Mendez Jr.

325th Glider Infantry Regiment : Colonel Lewis.
1/325th : Lieutenant-Colonel Boyd.

2/325th : Lieutenant-Colonel Swenson.
3/325th (ex-2/401st) : Lieutenant-Colonel Carrell.

82nd Airborne Division Artillery : Colonel March.
319th Glider FA Battalion : Lieutenant-Colonel Todd.
320th Glider FA Battalion : Lieutenant-Colonel Wright.
376th Parachute FA Battalion : Lieutenant-Colonel Griffith.
456th Parachute FA Battalion : Lieutenant-Colonel d'Alessio.
80th Airborne AA Battalion : Lieutenant-Colonel Singleton.
307th Airborne Engineer Battalion : Lieutenant-Colonel Palmer (taken prisoner on June 6 and replaced by Major Bedell on June 8).
307th Airborne Cie medical : Major Houston (killed on June 6 and replaced by Major Belden).
407th Airborne Quartermaster Company: Captain Mays
782nd Airborne Ordnance Maintenance Company: Captain Davis Jr
82nd Airborne HQ Company: Captain Claussen
82nd Airborne HQ Company: Lieutenant Nerf
82nd Airborne Reconnaissance Section: Lieutenant Demasi
82nd Airborne Military Police: Major McCollum
82nd Parachute Maintenance Company: Captain Griffin

Appendix V
ORDER OF BATTLE OF
THE US 101st AIRBORNE *SCREAMING EAGLES*

Commanding Officer: Major-General Taylor
Assistant Division Commander:
  Brigadier-General Pratt (killed on June 6)

Chief of Staff: Colonel Higgins

G 1. Lieutenant-Colonel Moore
G 2. Major Sommerfield
G 3. Lieutenant-Colonel Millener
G 4. Lieutenant-Colonel Kohls
G 5. Major Eberle
Pathfinders: Captain Lillyman
501st PIR: Colonel Johnson
1/501st: Lieutenant-Colonel Carroll (killed on June 6)
2/501st: Lieutenant-Colonel Ballard
3/501st: Lieutenant-Colonel Ewell

502nd PIR: Colonel Moseley (wounded on June 6)
1/502nd: Lieutenant-Colonel Cassidy
2/502nd: Lieutenant-Colonel Chappuis
3/502nd: Lieutenant-Colonel Cole

506th Parachute Infantry Regiment: Colonel Sink
1/506th : Lieutenant-Colonel Turner
2/506th : Lieutenant-Colonel Strayer
3/506th : Lieutenant-Colonel Wolverton (killed on June 6)
327th Glider Infantry Regiment: Colonel Wear
1/327th: Lieutenant-Colonel Salee
2/327th: Colonel Rouzie
3/327th (ex-1/401st): Lieutenant-Colonel Allen

101st Divisional Artillery: Brigadier-General McAuliffe
321st Glider Field Artillery Battalion:
  Lieutenant-Colonel Carmichael
907th Glider Field Artillery Battalion:
Lieutenant-Colonel Nelson
377th Parachute Field Artillery Battalion:
  Lieutenant-Colonel Weisberg
101st Airborne Signal Company: 1st Lieutenant Breen Jr
326th Airborne Medical Company: Major Barfield
326th Airborne Engineer Battalion:
Lieutenant-Colonel Pappas
Coy HQ and services: Captain Hogrefe

BIBLIOGRAPHY

Ouvrages

AMBROSE Stephen,
Pegasus Bridge June 6 1944,
George Allen & Unwin, 1984.

BEEVOR Antony,
D-Day et la Bataille de Normandie,
Calmann-Lévy, 2009.

BERNAGE Georges et FRANÇOIS Dominique,
Utah Beach, Sainte-Mère-Église,
Heimdal, 2004.

BERNAGE Georges,
Objectif Carentan, Heimdal, 2010.

BERNAGE Georges *et alii,*
Objectif Sainte-Mère-Église, Heimdal, 1993.

BERNAGE Georges *et alii,*
*Album Mémorial : Overlord, Jour J
en Normandie,* Heimdal, 1993.

BRANDO Mark,
*Vanguard of the Crusade. The 101st Airborne
Division in World War II,* Heimdal, 2012.

CARELL Paul,
Ils arrivent, Robert Laffont, 1961.

CLARK Lloyd,
Battle Zone Normandy, Orne Bridgehead,
Sutton Publishing Ltd, 2004.

CROOKENDEN Napier,
Dropzone Normandy, Charles Scribner's
Sons, New York, 1976.

D'ESTE Carlo,
Histoire du Débarquement, Perrin, 2013.

DE TREZ Michel,
*At the Point of no return. Pictorial History
of the American Paratroopers in the Invasion
of Normandy,* D-Day Publishing, 1994.

EISENHOWER Dwight D.,
Croisade en Europe, traduit de l'anglais par
Paule de Beaumont, Paris, Robert Laffont,
1949.

FOWLER Will,
Pegasus Bridge, Raid n° 11,
Osprey Publishing, 2010.

GOLLEY John,
La Nuit des canons de Merville,
Presses de la Cité, 1982.

GRIESSER Volker,
Les Lions de Carentan, Heimdal, 2006.

GUARD Julie (sous la direction de),
*Airborne, World War II Paratroopers
in Combat,* Osprey Publishing, 2007.

HART Russell A.,
*Clash of Arm., How the Allies won in
Normandy,* University of Oklahoma Press,
2004.

KEUSGEN Konrad von,
Pointe du Hoc, Heimdal, 2006.

KEUSGEN Konrad von,
Les Canons de Saint-Marcouf,
Heimdal, 2005.

LEFEBVRE Laurent,
Ils étaient à Utah Beach,
American D-Day Edition, 2004.

LUCK Hans von,
*Panzer Commander, The Memoirs
of Colonel Hans von Luck,*
A Dell Books, 1989.

MAGDELAINE Yann,
Atlas du Débarquement,
Éditions Ouest-France, 2012.

MARET Édouard et PARIS Claude,
*6 Juin, le Choc, Allemands et Américains
se souviennent des combats,*
Éditions Ouest-France, 2004.

MRAZEK James,
*Airborne Combat, The Glider War/Fighting
Gliders of WWII,* Stackpole Books, 2011.

POPPEL Martin,
*Heaven and Hell : The War Diary
of a German Paratrooper,* The History Press
Ltd, 2010.

QUELLIEN Jean,
Les Américains en Normandie,
OREP Éditions, 2012.

QUETEL Claude (sous la direction de),
  Dictionnaire du Débarquement,
  Éditions Ouest-France, 2011.
REARDON Mark,
  Defending Fortress Europe, The War Diary
  of the German 7th Army in Normandy,
  6 June to 26 July 1944, The Aberjona Press,
  2012.
RYAN Cornelius,
  Le Jour le plus long, Robert Laffont, 1960.
SAUNDERS Hilary St. George,
  The Red Beret, New English Library, 1955
  [Michael Joseph Ltd, 1950].
STAFFORD David,
  Ten Days to D-Day,
  Abacus, 2004 [Little, Brown, 2003].
THOMPSON R.W.,
  Le Jour J, ils débarquent, Marabout, 1970.
WEIGLEY Russell,
  Eisenhower's Lieutenants, The Campaigns
  of France and Germany, 1944-1945,
  Bloomington, Indiana University Press, 1981.
WHITLOCK Flint,
  If Chaos reigns, the near-disaster and
  ultimate triumph of the allied airborne
  forces on D-Day, June 6 1944,
  Casemate Publishers, 2011.
ZALOGA Steven, *Rangers*
  Lead the Way, Raid n° 1, Osprey Publishing,
  2009.

Periodicals
BERNAGE Georges,
La Nuit des paras, dans *Historica* n° 70,
  Heimdal, 2002.
BERNAGE Georges,
Les Paras du Jour J, dans *Historica* n° 71,
  Heimdal, 2002.
BOUCHERY Jean et DESCHODT
  Christophe, *Les Paras US de Normandie,*
  dans *Militaria Magazine* n° 22/23, 1987.
BRINK Denis Van den,
  Deux Ponts trop loin, dans *Normandie 1944*
  Magazine n° 2, 2012.
BRINK Denis Van den,
  Paras US à la pointe du Hoc, dans
  Normandie 1944 Magazine n° 4, 2012.
BUFFETAUT Yves,
  6 juin 1944, la Première Vague, dans
  Militaria Magazine, hors-série n° 12, 1993.
BUFFETAUT Yves,
  Paras sur la Normandie, dans *Militaria*
  Magazine, hors-série n° 54, 2004.
RONDEAU Benoît,
  Les Divisions d'infanterie dans l'enfer
  normand, dans *2e Guerre Mondiale*
  Magazine n° 2010.

Internet Sites:
www.6juin1944.com/
www.dday-overlord.com/
www.pegasusarchive.org/

Thanks

Thanks to Tanguy Le Sant and Benjamin Blondel,
for permission to use photographs from their collections to illustrate this work.
Thanks to Caroline Brou, for her iconographic research work.

Index

Les Editions Ouest-France thank the collectors and professionals
who have helped us with the illustrations, especially: Arromanches Militaria;
the Centre Historique des Parachutistes du 6 juin at St Côme-du-Mont;
Jean-Michel Selles of Static Line.

Editions OUEST-FRANCE

Rennes - Lille

Editeur : Matthieu Biberon
Coordination éditoriale : Caroline Brou
Conception graphique : Laurence Morvan, studio graphique des Editions Ouest-France
Cartographie Yann Magdelaine
Mise en pages : Brigitte Racine
Photogravure : graph&ti, Cesson-Sévigné (35)
Impression : Pollina à Luçon (85) - L68475B

© 2014, Editions Ouest-France,
Edilarge S. A., Rennes
ISBN : 978.2.7373.6361.0
N° d'éditeur : 7465.01.1,5.06.14
Dépôt légal : Juin 2014
Imprimé en France
www.editionsouestfrance.fr